SHOULDER
TO
SHOULDER

INSIGHTS INTO THE LIFE OF
THE APOSTLES

GENE GETZ

Published by Serendipity House Publishers
Nashville, Tennessee

International Standard Book Number: 1-57494-137-2

DEWEY: 225.92 SUBHD: APOSTLES--STUDY \ BIBLE. N.T.--STUDY \
MEN--RELIGIOUS LIFE

ACKNOWLEDGMENTS
Writing/Project Team: Joe Snider, Trent Butler, Ron Keck,
Scott Lee, and Rick Howerton

Scripture quotations are taken from the
Holman Christian Standard Bible,
© Copyright 2000 by Holman Bible Publishers. Used by permission.

To Zondervan Bible Publishers for permission to use the NIV text,
The Holy Bible, New International Bible Society. © 1973, 1978,
1984 by International Bible Society. Used by permission of
Zondervan Bible Publishers.

04 05 06 07 08 09 / 10 9 8 7 6 5 4 3 2 1

Nashville, Tennessee
1-800-525-9563
www.serendipityhouse.com

CONTENTS

SHOULDER TO SHOULDER

SHOULDER TO SHOULDER

A STUDY OF THE LIFE OF THE APOSTLES

They recklessly followed, denied, loved, and betrayed our Lord, still Jesus
saw fit to call them His Apostles and bestow on them the incredible
responsibility of spreading the gospel throughout the world. Each one,
brought a mosaic of backgrounds, experiences, personal strengths and
weaknesses and together they stood shoulder to shoulder and ultimately
became a band of brothers who would change the world.

HOW TO USE THIS BOOK

While this Bible study may be used individually, it is designed to be used
within the context of small groups. Each group meeting should include
all parts of the following "three-part agenda."

Ice-Breaker: Fun, history-giving questions are designed to warm the
group and to build understanding about the other group members. You
can choose to use all of the Ice-Breaker questions, especially if there is a
new group member who will need help in feeling comfortable with the
group.

One of the purposes of this book is to begin and to then solidify a
group. Therefore, getting to know one another and bonding together are
essential to the success of this course. The goal is to get better acquainted
during the Ice-Breaker part of each group session.

Bible Study: The heart of each meeting is the examination of the Bible.
The questions are open, discovery questions that lead to further inquiry.
Reference notes are provided to give everyone a "level playing field." The
emphasis is on understanding what the Bible says and applying the truth
to real life. The questions for each session build. There is always at least
one "going deeper" question provided. You should always leave time for
the last of the "questions for interaction." Should you choose, you can
use the optional "going deeper" question to satisfy the desire for the
challenging questions in groups that have been together for a while.

To help connect as a group, it is important for everyone to participate in the Bible Study. There are no right or wrong answers to the questions. The group members should strive to make all of the other group members feel comfortable during the Bible Study time. Because we all have differing levels of biblical knowledge, it is essential that we appreciate the personal context from which answers are given. We don't have to know much about Scripture to bring our own perspectives on the truths contained in the Scriptures. It is vital to keep encouraging all group members to share what they are observing as we work through these important Bible passages.

Caring Time: All study should point us to actions. Each session ends with prayer and direction in caring for the needs of the group members. You can choose between several questions.

Small groups help the larger body of Christ in many ways: caring for individuals, holding one another up in prayer, providing emotional support, and bringing new men into the body by reaching out to new guys. Each week it is important to remember to pray for those whom God would bring to your group.

How To Get The most out of this book

Begin by reviewing the following ground rules and talk about the importance of "sharing your story" (see below).

Ground Rules
• **Priority**: While you are in the group, you give the group meeting priority.

• **Participation**: Everyone participates, and no one dominates.

• **Respect**: Everyone is given the right to their own opinion, and all questions are encouraged and respected.

• **Confidentiality**: Anything that is said in the meeting is never repeated outside the meeting.

- **Empty Chair**: The group stays open to new men at every meeting.

- **Support**: Permission is given to call upon each other in time of need—even in the middle of the night.

- **Advice Giving**: Unsolicited advice is not allowed.

- **Mission**: We agree to do everything in our power to start a new group as our mission.

SHARING YOUR STORY

These sessions are designed for members to share a little of their personal lives each time the group meets. Through a number of special techniques, each member is encouraged to move from low risk, less personal sharing to higher risk responses. This helps develop community and facilitates caregiving.

Only when group members begin to share their own story does the group bond at levels deep enough for life-change to take place.

PETER: A HARD-HITTING SERVANT

WELCOME

In this study we will reflect on the lives of the apostles and what they can teach us. Though God will never choose one of us to be among those who laid the foundation of the church of Jesus Christ, He has chosen all of us to become men of God. These New Testament personalities point the way. The apostle Paul spoke for them all when he wrote, "Be imitators of me, as I also am of Christ" (1 Co 11:1).

ICE-BREAKER

We live in a culture that wants things now. We don't want to wait even for spiritual maturity. Two millennia ago, neither did the apostle Peter. In that respect Peter and we are like impatient children. God had to slow Peter down and get his attention through failure. Hopefully we can learn without as much pain.

1. When you were growing up, which of these was hardest for you to wait for? Why?
   a. Your birthday.
   b. Summer vacation.
   c. Christmas.
   d. Baseball/football/basketball season.
   e. Lunch.
   f. Other _____.

2. In your childhood neighborhood who was the natural leader who influenced all the other guys? What was the biggest mess he ever got you all into?

BIBLICAL FOUNDATION

The following Scriptures trace certain key encounters between Peter and Jesus that shaped this tough-minded businessman into one of God's greatest servants.

A New Name

[40] Andrew, Simon Peter's brother, was one of the two who heard John and followed Him. [41] He first found his own brother Simon and told him, "We have found the Messiah!" (which means "Anointed One"), [42] and he brought Simon to Jesus. When Jesus saw him, He said, "You are Simon, son of John. You will be called Cephas" (which means "Rock").

John 1:40-42

Penetrating Accountability Questions

[27] Then Jesus said to them, "All of you will fall, because it is written: I will strike the shepherd, and the sheep will be scattered. [28] But after I have been resurrected, I will go ahead of you to Galilee." [29] Peter told Him, "Even if everyone falls, yet I will not!" [30] "I assure you," Jesus said to him, "today, this very night, before the rooster crows twice, you will deny Me three times!" [31] But he kept insisting, "If I have to die with You, I will never deny You!" And they all said the same thing. [32] Then they came to a place named Gethsemane, and He told His disciples, "Sit here while I pray." [33] He took Peter, James, and John with Him, and He began to be horrified and deeply distressed. [34] Then He said to them, "My soul is swallowed up in sorrow—to the point of death. Remain here and stay awake." [35] Then He went a little farther, fell to the ground, and began to pray that if it were possible, the hour might pass from Him. [36] And He said, "Abba, Father! All things are possible for You. Take this cup away from Me. Nevertheless, not what I will, but what You will." [37] Then He came and found them sleeping. "Simon, are you sleeping?" He asked Peter. "Couldn't you stay awake one hour? [38] Stay awake and pray, so that you won't enter into temptation. The spirit is willing, but the flesh is weak."

Mark 14:27-38

Peter's Ultimate Failure

[54] They seized Him, led Him away, and brought Him into the high priest's house. Meanwhile Peter was following at a distance. [55] When they had lit a fire in the middle of the courtyard and sat down together, Peter sat among them. [56] When a servant saw him sitting in the firelight, and looked closely at him, she said, "This man was with Him too." [57] But he denied it: "Woman, I don't know Him!" [58] After a little while, someone else saw him and said, "You're one of them too!" "Man, I am not!" Peter said. [59] About an hour later, another kept insisting, "This man was certainly with Him, since he's also a Galilean." [60] But Peter said, "Man, I don't know what you're talking about!" Immediately, while he was still speaking, a rooster crowed.

Luke 22:54-60

Brokenness and Restoration

¹⁵ When they had eaten breakfast, Jesus asked Simon Peter, "Simon, son of John, do you love Me more than these?" "Yes, Lord," he said to Him, "You know that I love You." "Feed My lambs," He told him. ¹⁶ A second time He asked him, "Simon, son of John, do you love Me?" "Yes, Lord," he said to Him, "You know that I love You." "Shepherd My sheep," He told him. ¹⁷ He asked him the third time, "Simon, son of John, do you love Me?" Peter was grieved that He asked him the third time, "Do you love Me?" He said, "Lord, You know everything! You know that I love You." "Feed My sheep," Jesus said. . . . ¹⁹ After saying this, He told him, "Follow Me!"

John 21:15-17, 19b

PRINCIPLE DEVELOPMENT

Jesus took a tough-minded, successful businessman with a lot of raw talent and many rough edges and eventually changed him into a hard-hitting servant of God. It took time, but it happened. Underneath all that coarse exterior was a soft heart and a lot of love. Jesus changed him from the inside out.

Jesus also wants to change you.

PRINCIPLE I

No matter what your previous experience, Jesus Christ can use you to serve Him.

God specializes in transforming our hearts, redirecting our self-centered energy, and reshaping our raw talent and abilities to achieve His purposes in this world. He did this for Peter and, as we'll see, for the other men who followed Him. They were all different and unique. Only Judas Iscariot turned his back on Jesus.

Each of us is created in God's image but with distinct reflections of His unfathomable and indescribable personality. When one of us is born again, God doesn't change the individual's uniqueness. Instead He uses those unique qualities to create a special member of His church, the body of Christ. The church's diversity with unity is to continue, but under the control of the Holy Spirit. In the lessons to follow we'll see God's purposes unfold in the unique personality of each apostle.

As far as we know, Peter and his brother, Andrew, grew up in a good Jewish family. They had been taught the Law of Moses. The promise of the coming Messiah was not a strange concept to these men. When Peter began to follow Christ, it took several years for God to deal with his self-sufficiency, pride, and prejudice. Thankfully, the Lord could use him during this "growing up" period – when he "spoke like a child," "thought like a child," and "reasoned like a child" (1 Co 13:11). When Peter "became a man," God used him to the full.

Even when Peter failed Jesus the most, he didn't allow Satan to keep him in a state of defeat and despair. The important question is, What steps are you taking to forget "what is behind" and to set as your "goal the prize promised by God's heavenly call in Christ Jesus" (Php 3:13-14)?

PRINCIPLE 3

PREJUDICE IS ONE OF THE MOST DIFFICULT CHALLENGES MANY MEN FACE IN THEIR CHRISTIAN LIVES.

Five years after Pentecost, the Lord confronted Peter about his prejudice against Gentiles (Ac 10:1-36). When Peter obeyed the Lord and abandoned his bias, the rest of the church followed Peter's lead. It was one of his finest moments.

I was reared in a very exclusive religious community. I had been taught from a small child that our particular church group included the only true followers of Jesus Christ. Eventually, I realized this was not true and decided to leave this environment.

Ironically, as I look back, I have to acknowledge that it also took approximately five years to fully deal with the prejudice in my life. Don't be surprised, then, to discover that you may have prejudice lingering in your own soul. Don't be surprised if God allows you to experience a "crisis of faith" so you can deal with it.

Two things are certain: 1. No man is mature in Christ who is prejudiced against others; 2. God cannot use a man to the full if he allows this sin to continue and to affect his attitudes and actions toward others.

LESSON 1

QUESTIONS FOR INTERACTION

1. Which of these characteristics of Peter do you identify with most strongly? Why?
   a. Aggressive business leader.
   b. Spokesman for the group.
   c. Maker of bold promises he couldn't keep.
   d. Failure under pressure.
   e. Humble and repentant man when confronted.
   f. Struggler with stubborn prejudices.
   g. Other _____.

2. Which of these reasons do you think best explains why Jesus renamed Simon "The Rock"? Explain your choice.
   a. Jesus saw the solid strength inherent in Simon's personality.
   b. Jesus gave Simon a name that would challenge him to become a rock.
   c. Jesus used the name to predict how He would change Simon in spite of himself.
   d. Jesus used the new name to intrigue Simon and prepare him to accept a call to discipleship.

3. Why do you think Peter got so defensive when Jesus predicted he would deny Him? What are some better ways Peter might have responded?
   Self pride vs. humility

4. When Jesus asked Peter to pray with Him at Gethsemane, what personal benefit did Jesus hope Peter would gain from that prayer session?
   obedience - trust and obey

5. How do you think each of these affected Peter's denial of Jesus?
   a. His failure to pray in Gethsemane.
   b. His fear and confusion caused by Jesus' arrest.
   c. His instinct to save his hide.
   d. His failure to grasp the nature of Jesus' mission to die for the sins of the world.

6. What do you imagine Peter thought about his relationship with God after he had denied Jesus three times?

7. Jesus let Peter affirm his love for Him three times – the same number of times as he had denied Him. What do you think that accomplished for Peter?

8. At what points in these stories do you identify most closely with Peter? Why?

9. Which of these three principles for spiritual growth challenges you most? Why?

a. No matter what your previous experience, Jesus Christ can use you to serve Him.

b. It takes time to become the man God wants you to be.

c. Prejudice is one of the most difficult challenges many men face in their Christian lives.

GOING DEEPER

10. How has God used failure in your life to make you more humble and compassionate in your attitudes toward others? *wife's illness and death has lead to more compassion*

11. What do you sense God is trying to change about you now? What do you think He wants to accomplish as a result of this change?

patience,

CARING TIME

Peter was brash and impulsive, but he wasn't a fool. He was a natural leader whom Jesus prepared to play a key role in establishing the church. Jesus is at work preparing each of us for the role He has for us in His body.

1. What are some of the key elements in your education and background that you see God using in your service for Him?

teaching, facilitation, leadership

2. What prejudices did you learn in your family and community as you grew up? How do you think you can tell when God has overcome these in your life?

3. Pray that each man in the group will cooperate with God patiently and hopefully during the lifelong process of becoming the men God wants us to be.

NEXT WEEK

Next week we look at the apostle James. James appears second in the Gospel lists of the disciples, always after Peter. That had to grate on him, because James was a man bent on being the most important guy in the room. When we learn how Jesus molded this power-hungry man into a model of servanthood, we will have picked up a valuable life lesson.

SCRIPTURE NOTES

1:42 Cephas. The Aramaic name Cephas and the Greek name Peter both mean "rock." By renaming Simon upon first meeting him, Jesus challenged Simon to let Him transform his life and character. Although Peter often seemed unstable during Jesus' time with him (18:15-17, 25-27), after the ascension, Peter became the chief spokesman for the apostles and was later to be a leader in the early church (Ac 2:14).

NOTES ON MARK 14:27-38

14:32 Gethsemane. An olive orchard in an estate at the foot of the Mount of Olives just outside the eastern wall of Jerusalem. The name means literally "an olive press" (for making olive oil).

14:33 Peter, James, and John. Several times in the Gospels these three men accompany Jesus during a time of great significance. The recent rebuke by Peter (8:32) and self-centered request of James and John (10:35-40) did not damage their relationships with Jesus. Also note that each of these men had vowed to stay with Jesus through thick and thin (10:38-39; 14:29, 31). What Jesus asks them to share with Him here is not glory (which they wanted) but sorrow (which they kept denying would come). ***deeply distressed.*** Literally, filled with "shuddering awe." The human Jesus was filled with deep sorrow as the impact of submitting to His Father's will hit Him. Thus he could understand the great emotional swings Peter experienced.

14:34 stay awake. This was an invitation for Peter to join Jesus in preparation for the severe trial that was soon to come. While it expresses Jesus' desire for human companionship in His time of crisis, it also points out that Peter needed to prepare himself (vv. 37-41).

14:35 fell to the ground. This accents the emotional distress He was feeling. ***began to pray.*** This is the third time in Mark's Gospel that Jesus has been shown in prayer (1:35; 6:46). ***the hour.*** This word is often used to refer to an event that represents a crucial turning point in God's plan for a person or for the world (Mk 13:11,32; Jn 13:1; 16:32). In reference to Jesus, it specifically refers to His crucifixion (Jn 12:23).

14:36 Abba. This is how a child would address his father: "Daddy." This was not a title that was used in prayer in the first century. ***this cup.*** Like the word "hour," "cup" was also used in an image referring to the destiny God had in store for a person. ***Nevertheless, not what I will, but what You will.***

There was no doubt in Jesus' mind regarding what the Father's will was in this situation. While He pleaded that there might be another way, this sentence declares His commitment to follow the Father's lead regardless of the cost (14:42).

NOTES ON LUKE 22:54-60

22:54 the high priest. This was the spiritual head of Israel. On the Day of Atonement the high priest alone could enter the Most Holy Place and, with sprinkled blood, make atonement for the sins of the people. Caiaphas was the high priest before whom Jesus came (Mt 26:57).

22:59 since he's also a Galilean. This would have been known because of his accent. Peter lived in Capernaum, on the shores of the Sea of Galilee. He shared a house with his brother Andrew (Mk 1:29) and fished professionally. He may have been the foreman for the fleet of Zebedee, the father of James and John.

22:60 a rooster crowed. Roosters in Palestine might crow anytime between midnight and 3 a.m. (which was the reason that that particular watch was called "cock-crow"). Peter's denials therefore occurred in the very early morning hours.

NOTES ON JOHN 21:15-17, 19B

21:15 do you love Me more than these? This question is ambiguous, but Jesus is probably asking Peter if indeed he loves Him more than the others do as Peter indicated in 13:37. In asking this question, Jesus allows Peter the opportunity three times to pledge his love for Him. **Feed my lambs.** After each query about his love, Jesus calls Peter to demonstrate that love by being a "good shepherd" to Jesus' sheep. From this time Peter abandoned fishing and resumed leadership of the apostles (Ac 1:15). He preached the Pentecost sermon that launched the public ministry of the church (Ac. 2). He spearheaded the growth of the church in Jerusalem, Judea, and to Gentiles (Ac 2 – 10).

21:19b Follow Me! The important thing for Peter was to forget His failure, accept Jesus' forgiveness, and renew his commitment to be a Christ follower (12:26).

James: From Raucous Leader to Radical Follower

Last Week

Last week we looked at Peter, the leader of the band of apostles. We saw how the Lord transformed Simon, the natural take-charge leader, into Peter, the servant-leader. This session focuses on James, older brother of John and a man on a mission to be somebody in his world. Let's see what Jesus had in mind for a power freak.

Ice-Breaker

Most men have a competitive side that, on the one hand, pushes us to achieve good things but, on the other hand, tempts us to step on other people while we win.

1. Which of these brings out the competitor in you most intensely?
   a. An athletic contest.
   b. A business deal.
   c. An attractive woman.
   d. A public award.
   e. A fear of criticism.
   f. Other _____.

2. What's your favorite memory of a victory? When do you tend to think about it?

3. What's your worst memory of a loss? When do you tend to think about it?

Biblical Foundation

Jesus chose twelve apostles, but within that group He focused attention on three – Peter, James, and John. They're always listed in that order. James didn't like second billing, so he set out to change it. He didn't care if his plan made everyone else mad. Fortunately, Jesus never gave up on James. Jesus rebuked him and loved him until, in the end, James died for

Jesus. In that he was number one among the apostles.

A Firstborn Son

[16] [Jesus] appointed the Twelve: To Simon, He gave the name Peter; [17] and to James the son of Zebedee, and to his brother John, He gave the name "Boanerges" (that is, "Sons of Thunder").

Mark 3:16-17

Sons of Thunder

[51] When the days were coming to a close for Him to be taken up, He was determined to journey to Jerusalem. [52] He sent messengers ahead of Him, and on the way they entered a village of the Samaritans to make preparations for Him. [53] But they did not welcome Him, because He was determined to journey to Jerusalem. [54] When the disciples James and John saw this, they said, "Lord, do You want us to call down fire from heaven to consume them?" [55] But He turned and rebuked them, [56] and they went to another village.

Luke 9:51-56

Winning at Any Cost

[20] Then the mother of Zebedee's sons approached Him with her sons. She knelt down to ask Him for something. [21] "What do you want?" He asked her. "Promise," she said to Him, "that these two sons of mine may sit, one on Your right and the other on Your left, in Your kingdom."

Matthew 20:20-21

[35] Then James and John, the sons of Zebedee, approached Him and said, "Teacher, we want You to do something for us if we ask You." [36] "What do you want Me to do for you?" He asked them. [37] "Grant us," they answered Him, "that we may sit at Your right and at Your left in Your glory." [38] But Jesus said to them, "You don't know what you're asking. Are you able to drink the cup I drink, or to be baptized with the baptism I am baptized with?" [39] "We are able," they told Him. But Jesus said to them, "You will drink the cup I drink, and you will be baptized with the baptism I am baptized with. [40] But to sit at My right or left is not Mine to give, but it is for those for whom it has been prepared." [41] When the [other] 10 [disciples] heard this, they began to be indignant with James and John. [42] And Jesus called them over and said to them, "You know that those who are regarded as rulers of the Gentiles dominate them, and their men of high positions exercise power over them. [43] But it must not be like that among you. On the

contrary, whoever wants to become great among you must be your ser-vant, ⁴⁴ and whoever wants to be first among you must be a slave to all. ⁴⁵ For even the Son of Man did not come to be served, but to serve, and to give His life—a ransom for many."

Mark 10:35-45

The Ultimate Sacrifice
1 About that time King Herod cruelly attacked some who belonged to the church, ² and he killed James, John's brother, with the sword.

Acts 12:1-2

PRINCIPLE DEVELOPMENT

James came from a family that ran a business (Mt 4:21-22) and had political connections, knowing the high priest in Jerusalem (Jn 18:15-16). James enjoyed privilege among the apostles: he witnessed the heal-ing of Jairus' daughter (Mk 5:37) and the transfiguration of Jesus (Mt 17:1-2). James wanted to sit at Jesus' right hand in His Kingdom (Mk 10:35-37).

James felt the sting of Jesus' rebuke after he suggested calling fire down on a Samaritan village (Lk 9:55). He puzzled over the teaching that the greatest Christ-follower was the one who made himself a servant (Mk 10:43-45). He regretted falling asleep in Gethsemane when Jesus asked him to pray (14:32-41).

After the resurrection of Jesus and the coming of the Holy Spirit, James displayed a new heart and character that enabled him to give his life will-ingly for his Master (Ac 12:1-2).

PRINCIPLE I

NO MATTER WHAT OUR FAMILY BACKGROUND, JESUS CHRIST CAN MOLD OUR LIVES INTO HIS IMAGE.

All of us have been impacted by our family backgrounds. Unfortunately, many parents have not always been the best models. For example, many children today are reared in an environment that is intensely materialis-tic, as James' mother showed herself to be. In addition, more and more little boys grow up in families where they've never seen what God intended a good husband to be. They've never seen their father love their mother as God has commanded. They've not experienced love them-selves.

This is the primary reason God designed the church to be a "re-parenting" organism. When Christians love one another as Jesus taught His disciples to (Jn 13:34-35), the world will sit up and take notice. James' love became apparent when he died for Christ. Christians who have not learned what love is from their parents will experience it in their relationships with their pastors and their brothers and sisters in Christ.

PRINCIPLE 2

GOD IS LOOKING FOR DEDICATED MEN WITH NATURAL LEADERSHIP ABILITIES WHO WILL BECOME SERVANT LEADERS.

Initially, James used his God-created energy to be opportunistic and to further his own self-centered interests. When he was in the limelight on the Mount of Transfiguration, he was highly motivated. However, when he had to operate "behind the scenes" in the Garden of Gethsemane, he "went to sleep."

Jesus Christ wants to use our ego strength to achieve His goals. Men who follow Him must allow their God-created energies to be brought under the control of the Holy Spirit. Jesus wants to help us shed our self-centered pride and become humble but self-confident men, relying on God, while using all of the abilities He has given us.

PRINCIPLE 3

JESUS CHRIST WANTS TO USE OUR COMPETITIVE TENDENCIES TO BUILD HIS KINGDOM, NOT OUR OWN.

How can we do our best, have a winning spirit, "climb the corporate ladder," and yet be servants? This is not an easy question to answer, but I believe it's possible.

First, we need to be reminded that's it's not wrong to do our very best and to be rewarded. However, we must always reflect the fruit of the Holy Spirit in all of our relationships: "love, joy, peace, patience, kindness, goodness, faith, gentleness, self-control" (Gl 5:22-23).

Second, our motivation should always be to honor and glorify Jesus Christ. When we succeed, we must always remember to thank God and to use our new position to build His kingdom, not ours.

Third, we must never use our prominent position to lord it over others. In business, this means serving others and helping them to achieve their goals in the organization, in their families, and in their personal lives.

1. Which of these best captures your relationship to James, the driven first-born son?
   a. I'm a highly competitive first-born, too.
   b. I'm a firstborn but I'm not driven.
   c. I'm a middle child who competed with older siblings.
   d. I'm an ignored middle child.
   e. I'm a laid-back later child.
   f. I'm a peacemaking later child.
   g. Other _____.

2. James' father Zebedee owned a fishing business. His mother didn't hesitate to push her sons to achieve high positions. His family knew Caiaphas the high priest. How does your family background compare with that of James?

3. What explanations can you imagine for Jesus calling James and his brother John "Sons of Thunder"? What if "Thunder" refers to Zebedee rather than James and John?

4. As the older brother, James would have expected to sit at Jesus' right in the kingdom (Mk 10:37). What do you think James figured would happen to Peter, the current leader of the disciples?

5. Do you think James was surprised when the rest of the disciples got mad at him and John for asking for the chief positions in Jesus' kingdom (Mk 10:41)? Why or why not?

6. Both the Samaritan village incident and the request for prominence in the kingdom occurred as Jesus neared Jerusalem and the cross. Why was it necessary for Jesus to sharply rebuke James and his brother at this time? What would Jesus want James to remember after His resurrection and ascension?

7. How did James' martyrdom fulfill Jesus' prediction, "You will drink the cup I drink, and you will be baptized with the baptism I am baptized with" (Mk 10:39)?

8. What had to change in James' heart and mind for him to accept martyrdom instead of position and prestige as an apostle of Jesus Christ?

9. How can God use your competitive tendencies to build up Christ's church?

10. Which fruit of the Spirit (love, joy, peace, patience, kindness, goodness, faith, gentleness, self-control) do you need to cultivate in your life to keep your competiveness under God's control and in His service?

GOING DEEPER

11. What family characteristics (aggressive or passive) may you need to overcome to be a servant-leader to your family, your employer, or your church?

12. How do you tend to react to assertive leaders in the church? How can you distinguish between a godly and a selfish assertive leader?

CARING TIME

James ought to give us a lot of hope. He started out raucous, angry, judgmental, self-centered, and demanding. It took three years with Jesus to do the trick, but James turned out just fine. He became a radical follower to the extent that he faded into the background behind his younger brother John and behind Peter in the book of Acts. Then he gave his life without complaint.

1. James was a power-hungry man. How would you rate your hunger for power? Are you more concerned about being too aggressive or too passive? Why?

2. What particular expression of aggressiveness or passivity can this group hold you accountable to deal with?

3. Who in your world are you struggling to serve as God wants you to? How can we pray for you in regard to this situation?

NEXT WEEK

Next week we look at the apostle John, the younger brother of James. John survived long after the other apostles, so he may have been the youngest of the group. John enjoyed a special friendship with Jesus. In time that friendship transformed a self-centered young man into the apostle of love.

LESSON 2

SCRIPTURE NOTES

NOTES ON LUKE 9:51-56

9:52 Samaritans. Samaritans and Jews were bitter enemies. The Samaritans did not want anything to do with someone traveling to Jerusalem, since they believed the true place of worship was on a mountain in their province. James and John showed they wanted nothing to do with Samaritans.

9:54-55 do You want us to call down fire from heaven? Elijah once did this (2 Kg 1:9-12), so James and his brother may have seen it as an appropriate fate for those who treat Jesus shabbily. Jesus rebuked James for his loveless, vengeful attitude, which showed how little he still understood about the love of God. Do you have a group of people you would like to call down fire from heaven on?

NOTES ON MATTHEW 20:20-21; MARK 10:35-45

Mt 20:20 the mother of Zebedee's sons. In Mark's account, James and John approached Jesus directly. Matthew reveals that their mother tried to use her influence and womanly charm to prepare the way for her sons' appeal. Regardless of the role their mother played in this incident, it is clear that Jesus held them responsible for it (v. 24).

Mk 10:37 sit at Your right and at Your left in Your glory. They interpreted Jesus' heading toward Jerusalem as a sign that He would initiate His new kingdom in Jerusalem, over which He would reign as the new king of Israel.

10:38 drink the cup. This phrase means, "share the same fate." In the Old Testament, the cup is a metaphor for wrath (Ps 75:8; Is 51:17-22). ***baptism.*** The Old Testament uses the image of a deluge or flood overwhelming one as a metaphor for disaster (Ps 42:7; Is 43:2). Both the cup and the baptism refer to Jesus' coming suffering and death for the sins of the world. The path to the deadly cross is the only way to follow Jesus. James soon experienced that.

10:39 We are able. James too readily answered Jesus' question as to whether he could share Jesus' cup and baptism. He did not grasp what Jesus meant, thinking perhaps that He was referring to fellowship with Him. James' leadership would not be expressed through a position of authority but through suffering and death.

10:43 servant. Rather than become a master (and exercise authority), James had to become a follower (and meet the needs of others).

12:1 King Herod. This is Herod Agrippa I, the grandson of Herod the Great, who ruled when Jesus was born, and the nephew of Herod Antipas who governed Galilee during Jesus' ministry. Herod Agrippa I was popular with the Jews; some even wondered if he might be the Messiah who would free them from Rome. To further cultivate this popularity, he resumed the persecution of the church which had ceased upon Saul's conversion (9:31).

PERSONAL NOTES

LESSON 2

John: Arrogance Alleviated

Last Week

Last week we looked at James, the apostle who craved prominence. Jesus transformed angry, raucous, combative James into a radical follower who accepted a background role. This week we focus on John, James' younger brother. An arrogant guy, John, too, started out as a "Son of Thunder." Amazingly, Jesus turned John into the apostle of love.

Ice-Breaker

It's hard to imagine an angry person becoming known for being loving and lovable. Since we all struggle to some degree with our tempers, it's worth knowing how Jesus accomplished this transformation for the apostle John.

1. When you were growing up, who in your extended family was known as an angry person? How did family members deal with this person?

2. When you were a boy, what kinds of things made you mad?

3. Now that you're a man, what kinds of things make you mad?
   Bad Drivers

Biblical Foundation

The apostle John lived until the final years of the first century. Roughly seventy years elapsed between the call of John to be a disciple of Jesus and his death. John may have been no more than twenty years old when he dropped his nets and followed Jesus. He's a bit of a shadowy figure because he conceals his identity in the Gospel he wrote. Keep in mind that John was with Peter and James in many of the instances cited in the first two lessons.

A Plan that Backfired

[33] Then they came to Capernaum. When He was in the house, He asked them, "What were you arguing about on the way?" [34] But they were silent, because on the way they had been arguing with one another about who was the greatest.

³⁵ Sitting down, He called the Twelve and said to them. "If anyone wants to be first, he must be last of all and servant of all." ³⁶ Then He took a child, had him stand among them, and taking him in His arms, He said to them, ³⁷ "Whoever welcomes one little child such as this in My name welcomes Me. And whoever welcomes Me does not welcome Me, but Him who sent Me." ³⁸ John said to Him, "Teacher, we saw someone driving out demons in Your name, and we tried to stop him because he wasn't following us." ³⁹ "Don't stop him," said Jesus, "because there is no one who will perform a miracle in My name who can soon afterward speak evil of Me. ⁴⁰ For whoever is not against us is for us."

Mark 9:33-40

A Unique Relationship
²¹ When Jesus had said this, He was troubled in His spirit and testified, "I assure you: One of you will betray Me!"
²² The disciples started looking at one another—at a loss as to which one He was speaking about. ²³ One of His disciples, whom Jesus loved, was reclining close beside Jesus. ²⁴ Simon Peter motioned to him to find out who it was He was talking about. ²⁵ So he leaned back against Jesus and asked Him, "Lord, who is it?"

John 13:21-25

Total Confidence
²⁵ Standing by the cross of Jesus were His mother, His mother's sister, Mary the wife of Clopas, and Mary Magdalene. ²⁶ When Jesus saw His mother and the disciple He loved standing there, He said to His mother, "Woman, here is your son." ²⁷ Then He said to the disciple, "Here is your mother." And from that hour the disciple took her into his home.

John 19:25-27

Learning to Love
⁷ Dear friends, let us love one another, because love is from God, and everyone who loves has been born of God and knows God. ⁸The one who does not love does not know God, because God is love. ⁹God's love was revealed among us in this way: God sent His One and Only Son into the world so that we might live through Him. ¹⁰ Love consists in this: not that we loved God, but that He loved us and sent His Son to be the propitiation for our sins. ¹¹ Dear friends, if God loved us in this way, we also must love one another. ¹² No one has ever seen God. If we love one another, God remains in us and His love is perfected in us.

1 John 4:7-12

LESSON 3

PRINCIPLE DEVELOPMENT

The same strong parents who influenced James to be a power freak left their fingerprints on the character of John. He, too, was a Son of Thunder, ready to call down fire on the Samaritan village that excluded Jesus. He, too, asked for a seat at Jesus' side in His kingdom.
John was younger and more sensitive than his older brother James. His sensitivity set the direction for the transformation Jesus would work in him. John cherished the friendship Jesus offered him and gained the seat of companionship next to the Master, if not the seat of power and prestige he coveted. Youth gave John's legs speed to outrun Peter to the empty tomb on Easter morning where he looked around at all the evidence "and believed" (Jn 20:8).

PRINCIPLE 1

JESUS CHRIST LOVES ALL OF US UNCONDITIONALLY, NO MATTER HOW SELFISH AND ARROGANT WE MAY BE.

John was an arrogant, self-centered man who had a terrible temper. Jesus, however, loved him dearly even when he was obnoxious and self-serving. John not only understood personally what it means to be loved unconditionally, but he saw this happen to others. He witnessed first-hand that the Lord could save a self-righteous Pharisee named Nicodemus (Jn 3:1-21). He saw Jesus transform an immoral Samaritan woman when she put her faith in the Savior (4:1-42). He also looked on in amazement when Thomas, a real skeptic, proclaimed, "My Lord and my God!" (20:28).

Jesus Christ loves you no matter what your religious or pagan background, no matter what your sin or your unbelief. If you put your faith in the Lord Jesus Christ and believe that He died and rose again for you personally, you'll pass from death to life (3:36; 5:24).

PRINCIPLE 2

JESUS CHRIST WANTS TO HAVE A UNIQUE, ONGOING, AND RECIPROCAL LOVE RELATIONSHIP WITH ALL HIS CHILDREN.

When Jesus walked this earth, He had a special relationship with John. Once He atoned for sin and ascended to heaven, He made it possible for all of us to have that kind of relationship with Him.

Today Jesus Christ has no favorites. He loves us all the same. In His humanity He loved John in a special way. But as the great high priest and mediator who now sits at the right hand of God the Father, He shows no partiality. He has no favorites. He desires to have a warm, loving relationship with each of His children.

Jesus wants us to be able to comprehend His love with our minds and feel His love in our hearts. God the Father also wants all of us, no matter how good or bad our experiences with our biological fathers, to be able to relate to Him, not just with head knowledge but with heart experience. He is our heavenly Father, and He wants us to walk with Him day by day in deep and abiding friendship.

PRINCIPLE 3

JESUS CHRIST HAS MADE IT POSSIBLE FOR US TO BE A PART OF A DYNAMIC COMMUNITY OF LOVE THAT NOT ONLY MEETS OUR NEEDS BUT DEMONSTRATES TO THE WORLD THAT JESUS CHRIST IS THE INCARNATE SON OF GOD.

When Jesus walked among men and women working miracles, He was demonstrating His deity. When he returned to heaven, He left His people to demonstrate that He was one with the Father. On the evening before He died, Jesus illustrated through the foot-washing experience that His disciples should love one another as He had loved them (Jn 13:34-35). Following the foot-washing, Jesus prayed for unity among His disciples. As He walked with them geographically toward the Kidron Valley, He led them spiritually toward the cross. The apostle John heard Jesus tell the Father, "I pray not only for these, but also for those who believe in Me through their message. May they all be one, just as You, Father, are in Me and I am in You. May they also be one in Us, so that the world may believe You sent Me" (Jn 17:20-21).

QUESTIONS FOR INTERACTION

1. Through John's close friendship with Jesus, He became an expert on love. What do you want your friendship with Jesus to make you an expert in? Why?

2. Why did Jesus object to John rebuking the person driving out demons in Jesus' name (Mk 9:22-40)?

3. How do you think Jesus would have liked John to respond to the person driving out demons in His name?

4. In the story about who would betray Jesus, what shows John's special intimacy with Jesus (Jn 13:21-25)?

5. Jesus entrusted His mother to John. How many different emotions can you imagine John experienced at that moment at the foot of the cross?

6. What practical lessons about love do you think John learned from caring for Mary after Jesus returned to heaven?

7. According to 1 John 4:7-12, how did John come to know what love is? Is there another way to learn about love? Have you learned about love from God's love for you and His presence in you?

8. How does John say that we are to express the love of God?

9. John's close friendship with Jesus transformed his life and character. Which of these statements best captures how your relationship with Jesus tends to work?
   a. Jesus is the Boss, so I do what I'm told.
   b. Jesus is the Judge, so I don't want to make Him mad.
   c. Jesus is for Sunday, so I ignore Him through the week.
   d. Jesus is unpredictable, so I worry about what He'll let happen to me next.
   e. Jesus is my Friend, so we talk about everything and He guides me.
   f. Other _____

10. If God ran a check on your personality for characteristics that could interfere with love, which ones do you think He might red flag?
    impatience

GOING DEEPER

11. What relationship that God has put in your life (like Jesus put Mary in John's life) has taught you the most about love? What specifically have you learned?

12. How can the relationships we build in this group express God's love to the watching world?

LESSON 3

CARING TIME

The apostle John models for us a life changed through friendship with the Lord Jesus. John didn't start following Jesus to learn about love. Jesus took a liking to John and showed him special attention. He has taken the same liking to each of His followers ever since.

1. If Jesus is your close friend, how should that affect the way you respond to what He says through the Bible?

2. If Jesus is your close friend, how should that affect the way you talk with Him in prayer?

3. If Jesus is your close friend, how can you show His love in your family, in your church, and in your workplace? Pray for members of your group to be ready and able to desplay the love of Christ, your Friend, in all these relationships this week.

NEXT WEEK

Next week we move beyond Peter, James, and John, the inner circle of Jesus' disciples, to meet Andrew. Andrew was Peter's brother. In fact, Andrew brought Peter to Jesus. He had followed John the Baptist as a disciple and may have been the first of the Twelve to attach himself to Jesus. Andrew, however, wasn't a forceful personality. He found his place in the background as a quiet, respected encourager of others.

NOTES ON MARK 9:33-40

9:34 greatest. Once again John missed the point. In the face of Jesus' teaching about suffering and death, John was concerned about his position and personal power.

9:38 someone driving out demons in Your name. In exorcism, the power of the name dominated. This unnamed exorcist is an example of one of His followers who is to be welcomed (thus illustrating the point Jesus made in v. 37).

NOTES ON JOHN 13:21-25

13:21 troubled in His spirit. In all the references to Jesus being troubled, the fact of death disturbed Him (11:33; 12:27).

13:23 One of His disciples, whom Jesus loved: This is the first mention of a beloved disciple who appears several times in these final chapters (19:26-27; 20:2; 21:7, 20). This disciple is John, who wrote the Gospel. From a human point of view, Jesus had a deep friendship with John. As the son of God he loved all the apostles the same. ***reclining close beside Jesus.*** Formal meals were eaten while the participants reclined on their left side upon couches arranged in a horseshoe shape around a common table. John reclined with his back to Jesus. To speak to Jesus, John would lean back on his left shoulder and look up into Jesus' face.

NOTES ON JOHN 19:25-27

19:25 His mother, His mother's sister, Mary the wife of Clopas, and Mary Magdalene. With her sister and two friends, Mary watched her oldest son Jesus die a horrible death normally reserved for criminals. She had been told that her status as mother of the Son of God would make her blessed (Lk 1:42), but she no doubt did not feel very "blessed" at this point. Instead, a sword had pierced her soul (2:35).

19:26 the disciple He loved. It appears that by this time Joseph, Mary's husband, was dead. As the oldest son, Jesus would have assumed the responsibility of caring for His mother (13:23). Jesus chose John to be Mary's guardian. John seems to have interpreted his selection by Jesus as based on His love for him.

NOTES ON 1 JOHN 4:7-12

4:10 the propitiation for our sins. The word propitiation has to do with the removal of divine wrath. Jesus' death is the means that turns God's wrath from the sinner (see Rm 3:25; 2 Co 5:21; 2Jn 2:2).

Personal Notes

Andrew: Less Is More

Last Week

Last week we looked at John, the third of the inner circle of Jesus' disciples. We learned from his example that an arrogant, self-promoting young man can become a champion of love if he maintains a close personal relationship with Jesus. This week we turn our attention to Andrew who introduced his brother Peter to Jesus. Andrew was, in fact, the first of the apostles who discovered and believed in the Lord.

Ice-Breaker

Andrew must have lived in Simon Peter's shadow all his life. Peter was an outspoken man of action and a natural leader. Andrew seems to have been more introspective and given to following strong leaders. Even when Andrew led the way to Jesus, it wasn't long before Peter was in charge.

1. When you were a boy, whom did you look up to and hang around with in an effort to be like him? Was that a positive or negative experience? Why?

2. When you were in high school, were you primarily a leader or a follower? Give an experience that illustrates this.

3. Describe a memory of someone getting or taking credit for something you did? How did that make you feel?

Biblical Foundation

Andrew may have been the most spiritual of the apostles. He followed John the Baptist before he followed Jesus (Jn 1:35-36,40). But after he spent a day with the Lord, he believed Jesus was the Messiah. He immediately brought his brother Simon (Peter) to meet him (vv. 40-42). Andrew was officially the second disciple Jesus selected (Mk 1:16-17), but he is usually listed fourth among the Twelve (Mk 3:16-18). Occasionally the inner circle of disciples included Peter, James, John, and Andrew (Mk 13:3-4). Usually, however, Andrew had to be content as a behind-the-scenes Christ-follower.

An Eager Follower

³⁵ Again the next day, John was standing with two of his disciples.
³⁶ When he saw Jesus passing by, he said, "Look! The Lamb of God!"
³⁷ The two disciples heard him say this and followed Jesus. ³⁸ When
Jesus turned and noticed them following Him, He asked them, "What
are you looking for?" They said to Him, " Rabbi" (which means
"Teacher"), "where are You staying?" ³⁹ "Come and you'll see," He
replied. So they went and saw where He was staying, and they stayed
with Him that day. It was about 10 in the morning. ⁴⁰ Andrew, Simon
Peter's brother, was one of the two who heard John and followed Him.
⁴¹ He first found his own brother Simon and told him, "We have found
the Messiah!" (which means "Anointed One"), ⁴² and he brought
[Simon] to Jesus.

John 1:35-42a

Melting into the Background

¹⁶ As He was passing along by the Sea of Galilee, He saw Simon and
Andrew, Simon's brother. They were casting a net into the sea, since
they were fishermen.¹⁷ "Follow Me," Jesus told them, "and I will make
you fish for people!" ¹⁸ Immediately they left their nets and followed
Him. ¹⁹ Going on a little farther, He saw James the son of Zebedee and
his brother John. They were in their boat mending their nets.
²⁰ Immediately He called them, and they left their father Zebedee in
the boat with the hired men and followed Him. . . .
²⁹ As soon as they left the synagogue, they went into Simon and
Andrew's house with James and John. ³⁰ Simon's mother-in-law was
lying in bed with a fever, and they told Him about her at once. ³¹ So
He went to her, took her by the hand, and raised her up. The fever left
her, and she began to serve them.
³² When evening came, after the sun had set, they began bringing to
Him all those who were sick and those who were demon-possessed.
³³ The whole town was assembled at the door, ³⁴ and He healed many
who were sick with various diseases and drove out many demons. But
He would not permit the demons to speak, because they knew Him.
³⁵ Very early in the morning, while it was still dark, He got up, went
out, and made His way to a deserted place. And He was praying there.
³⁶ Simon and his companions went searching for Him. ³⁷ They found
Him and said, "Everyone's looking for You!"

Mark 1:16-20, 29-37

Helping with Philip

⁵ Therefore, when Jesus looked up and noticed a huge crowd coming

toward Him, He asked Philip, "Where will we buy bread so these people can eat?" [6] He asked this to test him, for He Himself knew what
He was going to do. [7] Philip answered, "Two hundred denarii worth
of bread wouldn't be enough for each of them to have a little."
[8] One of His disciples, Andrew, Simon Peter's brother, said to Him,
[9] "There's a boy here who has five barley loaves and two fish—but
what are they for so many?"
[10] Then Jesus said, "Have the people sit down."

There was plenty of grass in that place, so they sat down. The men
numbered about 5,000. [11] Then Jesus took the loaves, and after giving
thanks He distributed them to those who were seated—so also with
the fish, as much as they wanted.

John 6:5-11

[20] Now some Greeks were among those who went up to worship at the
festival. [21] So they came to Philip, who was from Bethsaida in Galilee,
and requested of him, "Sir, we want to see Jesus."
[22] Philip went and told Andrew; then Andrew and Philip went and
told Jesus. [23] Jesus replied to them, "The hour has come for the Son
of Man to be glorified. . . ."

John 12:20-23

PRINCIPLE DEVELOPMENT

Andrew was a religious man. Spiritual issues had impelled him to follow
John the Baptist while Peter, James, and John hauled fish out of the Sea
of Galilee and made money. It probably didn't surprise Andrew that his
brother Peter became the most prominent apostle in Jesus' band of followers. After all, he had walked in Peter's shadow all his life. Watching
James and John move ahead of him in the pecking order may have been
harder to take for Andrew.

Andrew probably struggled with the anger and power consciousness
of the Sons of Thunder. Jesus, however, saw qualities in the more worldly
fishermen that He chose to nurture and develop. Andrew slipped to
number four on the roster of disciples. Still, Andrew played a very
important role among the apostles, finding ways to help other people
find Jesus. In many respects during the time the other apostles traveled
with Jesus, Andrew illustrates Jesus' lesson on servanthood more than the
others. (John 13:12-15)

PRINCIPLE 1

JESUS CHRIST NEEDS MULTIPLIED MILLIONS OF MEN LIKE ANDREW,
TRUE SERVANT-LEADERS WHO WILL BUILD HIS CHURCH.

Few of us men are willing to step aside when we see someone emerge
who has more leadership abilities and skills than we do. It's hard for us to
imagine that less can be more. We've seen earlier that James and John
faced this situation. When the Holy Spirit transformed their lives and
they finally understood the spiritual nature of Christ's kingdom, both of
them willingly took a back seat to Peter.

Andrew faced the same challenge but to an even greater degree. He
had not only played "second fiddle" all his life to his brother, Peter, but
now he had to watch James and John move ahead of him. What is amazing is that he accepted his role, seemingly with a positive attitude.
Perhaps Andrew learned this powerful lesson from John the Baptist. Prior
to his imprisonment, John was baptizing in one place while Jesus was
baptizing nearby in another. Some of John's disciples came and reported
that people were flocking to Jesus. Andrew, who at that time was a disciple of John, no doubt overheard John's meek and humble reply: "He
must increase, but I must decrease" (Jn 3:30).

PRINCIPLE 2

SOME OF THE STRONGEST AND MOST EFFECTIVE LEADERS IN CHRISTIAN
MINISTRY ARE MEN WHO ARE NOT UP-FRONT BUT WHO ARE OPERATING
BEHIND THE SCENES.

In many respects, Andrew was this kind of man. If he hadn't been there,
he would have been terribly missed. Yet, even though he was there, he
often went unnoticed. So it is today in God's work. Support people are
very important. They're the people who help prominent leaders succeed.
In fact, we need far more "Andrews" than we do "Peters." Putting it
another way, some ministries fail because there are too many "chiefs" and
not enough "Indians." When we practice this aspect of servant leadership,
we are applying in a very special way what Paul taught the Roman
Christians: to honor others above ourselves (Rm 12:10 NIV).

WHEN PEOPLE WE INTRODUCE TO CHRIST BECOME STRONG, SUCCESS-
FUL LEADERS, WE WILL SHARE IN THEIR REWARDS.

When Peter preached on the Day of Pentecost, thousands put their faith in Jesus Christ. However, the Lord used Andrew to introduce Peter to Jesus. I'm confident that when both men stand before the judgment seat of Christ and receive rewards for their faithfulness, Andrew will share in all of Peter's accomplishments.

Paul made this principle clear when he thanked the Philippians for their monetary gifts when he was in prison. He reminded them that their investment in the ministry work of others was yielding dividends in their accounts in heaven (Php 4:17). Never be discouraged when your spiritual children surpass you in maturity or ministry. Learn a lesson from Andrew and Peter.

QUESTIONS FOR INTERACTION

1. Which of the following song titles best captures how you would have responded if you had fallen from number one to number four in the ranks of the disciples?
   a. Don't It Make My Brown Eyes Blue?
   b. I Shot the Sheriff.
   c. Walk Like a Man.
   d. You're a Mean One, Mr. Grinch.
   e. Amazing Grace
   f. Heartbreak Hotel
   g. Other _____.

2. How did Andrew initially reach the decision that Jesus was the Messiah (Jn 1:35-41)?

3. What do you conclude about Andrew from the way he immediately brought his brother to meet Jesus (Jn 1:41-42)?

4. In the account of the day Jesus formally called Andrew to become His disciple, what evidence do you find that Andrew was already moving into the background (Mk 1:16-39)?

5. How would you contrast the responses of Philip and Andrew to Jesus' question about feeding the multitude (Jn 6:7-8)?

6. Why do you think Andrew bothered telling Jesus about the boy's five loaves and two fish?

7. Why do you suppose Philip wanted Andrew's support before taking the Greek seekers to Jesus (Jn 12:20-22)?

8. What qualities do these passages illustrate or hint at that made Andrew a respected, indispensable behind-the-scenes apostle?

9. Would you say that God has wired your personality and gifted you to be a behind-the-scenes kind of guy, or are you more of an up-front sort? What kinds of things make you think that?

GOING DEEPER

10. If you are a behind-the-scenes follower of Jesus, how do you keep from losing motivation? How do you keep the up-front types from taking advantage of you?

11. If you are an up-front kind of disciple, how much attention do you pay to the behind-the-scenes people who support you? How could you express more appreciation? Do you need to move them more up front sometimes?

CARING TIME

The apostle Andrew showed a lot of character when he moved into the background without bitterness or complaint. Too often men get defensive and uncooperative when others succeed at their expense. We need to support and encourage one another whatever our level of public prominence.

1. Can you name someone who reminds you of Andrew? How?

2. Who in our church could we honor as a faithful, behind-the-scenes Andrew? How should we honor him/her?

3. What challenges are you facing in being supportive of someone else that we can pray with you about?

NEXT WEEK

Next week we consider the character of Philip, the apostle often linked with Andrew. Like Andrew, pragmatic Philip was someone Jesus could depend on. Unlike Andrew, Philip wrestled with his faith. He didn't pretend to be more spiritual than he was. When he didn't understand, he asked blunt questions, and Jesus gave him blunt answers. Jesus was glad Philip asked. He's also glad when we question Him and respond to His answers.

NOTES ON JOHN 1:35-42

1:38 *What are you looking for?* Jesus wanted to know what motivated Andrew and his friend (Jn 2:24; 6:26). ***Rabbi.*** Rabbis were teachers who gathered disciples around them. ***staying.*** This is the same word translated in verse 33 as "resting on" or remaining on. It hints that the concern in this question ("Where are you staying?") is on Jesus' true dwelling place. In this Gospel, recognition of Jesus' identity is tied up with recognizing where He is from and where He is going (8:21; 9:30; 14:2-6).

1:39 *Come and you'll see.* Jesus invited Andrew to enter into the journey of discipleship with Him.

1:41 *We have found the Messiah!* This is the fourth title ascribed to Jesus in this section (vv. 29, 33-34). Each title invites us to see Jesus in a new light and relate to Him in a new manner.

NOTES ON MARK 1:16-20, 29-39

1:20 *the hired men.* James and John came from a middle-class family. Their father Zebedee had men working for him and had boats with which to trawl the lake for fish. (Luke 5:3,10 says that Simon also had a fishing boat which may have actually belonged to Zededee.)

1:29 *into Simon and Andrew's house.* Simon and his wife shared a house with Andrew. Jesus and the disciples most likely went there for a meal, since the main Sabbath meal was served immediately after the synagogue service.

1:30 *Simon's mother-in-law.* For Simon Peter's marriage see also 1 Corinthians 9:5.

1:31 *The fever left her.* This was a real, immediate cure. She suffered none of the weakness that normally follows when a fever breaks.

1:35 Simon and his companions. By this point in the story, Andrew has faded into the anonymity of one of Simon's companions.

NOTES ON JOHN 6:5-11

6:9 five barley loaves. The poor used barley bread because it was less expensive than wheat. From Luke 11:15 we may assume that three loaves were normally a meal. At most the boy had provisions for two people. **what are they for so many?** The question Andrew and Philip asked is similar to Moses' response when the people clamored for meat (Nm 11:22).

NOTES ON JOHN 12:20-23

12:20 some Greeks. These would be Gentile converts to Judaism such as the men described in Acts 8:27; 10:2.

12:23 The hour has come. Throughout the Gospel, the author has anticipated this time (2:4; 7:6; 8:20). From here on Jesus speaks of how the "hour has come" (13:1; 17:1): this is the time of His glorification which is initiated by His death (Jn 12:27-28).

LESSON 4

Philip: Passionate Pragmatism

LESSON 5

Last Week

Last week we discovered that Andrew was a spiritually-minded apostle whose retiring personality removed him from prominence in the band of disciples. We saw how he willingly allowed Peter, James, and John to form the apostolic leadership core, allowing less to become more. Andrew was a trusted, valued behind-the-scenes player. The apostle Philip often appeared alongside Andrew. This week we look at this sensible, pragmatic fellow.

Ice-Breaker

Philip and Andrew were friends who looked at life differently. Philip questioned what he heard and wanted evidence. Andrew readily embraced new ideas and trusted what he heard from sources he held to be reliable. They probably complemented one another. Andrew challenged Philip to try new things; Philip cautioned Andrew to be careful.

1. Were you a risk-taker or a cautious type when you were a boy? Give an example.

2. If you were a risk-taker, who in your circle of friends was the cautious type who told you to be careful? If you were a cautious type, who among your friends dared you to take chances?

3. In either case, was your friend from item 2 a good or bad influence? How?

Biblical Foundation

When John the Baptist pointed Jesus out as "the Lamb of God, who takes away the sin of the world" (Jn 1:29), he lost two disciples. They followed Jesus (1:37). Andrew was one (1:40). In all likelihood, Philip was the other. The two of them appeared together on other occasions in John's Gospel (6:5-9; 12:20-22). Like Andrew, Philip immediately brought somebody else, in his case Nathanael, to meet Jesus (1:45). There the similarity to Andrew stopped. Philip often measured things with his intellect, wanting to know it really worked. While Andrew readily believed and grew in his faith, Philip struggled mightily. But after asking hard questions and struggling with his doubt, he became a true believer.

A Stickler for Detail

[35] Again the next day, John was standing with two of his disciples. [36] When he saw Jesus passing by, he said, "Look! The Lamb of God!" [37] The two disciples heard him say this and followed Jesus. [38] When Jesus turned and noticed them following Him, He asked them, "What are you looking for?" They said to Him, "Rabbi" (which means "Teacher"), "where are You staying?" [39] "Come and you'll see," He replied. So they went and saw where He was staying, and they stayed with Him that day. It was about 10 in the morning.... [43] The next day He decided to leave for Galilee. Jesus found Philip and told him, "Follow Me!" [44] Now Philip was from Bethsaida, the hometown of Andrew and Peter. [45] Philip found Nathanael and told him, "We have found the One Moses wrote about in the law (and so did the prophets): Jesus the son of Joseph, from Nazareth!" [46] "Can anything good come out of Nazareth?" Nathanael asked him. "Come and see," Philip answered.

John 1:35-39, 43-46

A Realist about Problems

[5] Therefore, when Jesus looked up and noticed a huge crowd coming toward Him, He asked Philip, "Where will we buy bread so these people can eat?" [6] He asked this to test him, for He Himself knew what He was going to do. [7] Philip answered, "Two hundred denarii worth of bread wouldn't be enough for each of them to have a little." [8] One of His disciples, Andrew, Simon Peter's brother, said to Him, [9] "There's a boy here who has five barley loaves and two fish—but what are they for so many?" [10] Then Jesus said, "Have the people sit down." There was plenty of grass in that place, so they sat down. The men numbered about 5,000. [11] Then Jesus took the loaves, and after giving thanks He distributed them to those who were seated—so also with the fish, as much as they wanted.

John 6:5-11

A Pragmatist Reaching for Faith

[1] "Your heart must not be troubled. Believe in God; believe also in Me. [2] In My Father's house are many dwelling places; if not, I would have told you. I am going away to prepare a place for you. [3] If I go away and prepare a place for you, I will come back and receive you to Myself, so that where I am you may be also. [4] You know the way where I am going." [5] "Lord," Thomas said, "we don't know where You're going.

How can we know the way?" ⁶ Jesus told him, "I am the way, the truth, and the life. No one comes to the Father except through Me. ⁷ "If you know Me, you will also know My Father. From now on you do know Him and have seen Him." ⁸ "Lord," said Philip, "show us the Father, and that's enough for us." ⁹ Jesus said to him, "Have I been among you all this time without your knowing Me, Philip? The one who has seen Me has seen the Father. How can you say, 'Show us the Father'? ¹⁰ Don't you believe that I am in the Father and the Father is in Me? The words I speak to you I do not speak on My own. The Father who lives in Me does His works. ¹¹ Believe Me that I am in the Father and the Father is in Me. Otherwise, believe because of the works themselves."

John 14:1-11

PRINCIPLE DEVELOPMENT

Philip, Andrew's friend, seems to have been a skeptical man who looked for material, practical solutions to problems. He didn't have Andrew's eager response to Jesus after John the Baptist pointed out the Lamb of God (Jn 1:40-41). He made measured statements about Jesus using Old Testament terminology and genealogical data rather than expressions of personal faith (v. 45). He stumbled over Jesus' challenge to feed the five thousand (6: 5-7) and wanted evidence of His assertion that He was going to the Father (14:6-8).

Philip raised questions countless others have raised through the centuries. In the process of reaching Philip, Jesus clarified issues that have helped his spiritual "descendants" through the ensuing centuries. Once he was convinced, Philip's pragmatic character made him a strong, stabilizing influence among the apostles as they spread the gospel.

PRINCIPLE 1

IN VIEW OF HIS CLAIMS, JESUS CHRIST CANNOT BE JUST A GREAT MORAL TEACHER.

When Philip first met Jesus, he concluded that he and Andrew had "found the One of whom Moses wrote in the law (and so did the prophets): Jesus the son of Joseph, from Nazareth" (Jn 1:45). He stated in no uncertain terms that Jesus fulfilled the messianic prophecies of the Old Testament. However, he assigned Jesus human parentage. He had not considered that Jesus might be divine. The idea that Jesus would become the sacrifice that would pay for his sins hadn't crossed Philip's mind.

Philip wanted a teacher to follow in place of John the Baptist. He didn't know Jesus had to be his Savior, nor did he realize what it would mean to call Jesus, Lord. Philip struggled with his native pragmatism and skepticism whenever he had to face another evidence that Jesus was more than a great teacher.

In the end, Philip reached certainty that Jesus was one with the Father, but he had to bump heads with Jesus before he could grasp that startling truth (Jn 14:8-11). Philip succeeded because he was a sincere seeker. He could not deny the logic inherent in all he learned about the Lord Jesus during three years of discipleship.

PRINCIPLE 2

EVERY PERSON WHO SINCERELY AND HUMBLY SEARCHES TO KNOW WHO JESUS CHRIST REALLY IS WILL DISCOVER A SATISFACTORY ANSWER.

The key words in this principle are sincerely, humbly, and search. When Moses recorded the law of God for Israel, he foresaw a time when God's people would deny Him and "worship man-made gods of wood and stone" (Dt 4:28). This would bring judgment and captivity in a foreign land. This promise was attached to that prediction:

"But from there, you will search for the Lord your God, and you will find [Him} when you seek Him with all your heart and all your soul" (Dt 4:29).

In Philip's hearing Jesus elaborated on this same promise:

"So I say to you, keep asking, and it will be given to you. Keep searching, and you will find. Keep knocking, and the door will be opened to you. For everyone who asks receives, and the one who searches finds, and to the one who knocks, the door will be opened" (Lk 11:9-10).

Philip's hardheaded pragmatism kept asking, searching, and knocking. He may have been skeptical, but he also was sincere and humble enough to be honest. Philip's faith eventually latched hold of the truth about Jesus because he didn't let personal pride prevent his knee from bending before the Son of God.

PRINCIPLE 3

DOUBTS AND QUESTIONS ARE NORMAL, EVEN FOR TRUE CHRISTIANS, PARTICULARLY AT CERTAIN POINTS IN OUR LIVES.

All of the apostles demonstrated that doubt and unbelief are normal weaknesses in all human beings. Philip's steely-eyed realism brought his doubt and unbelief to the fore more obviously than all the other apostles, except for Thomas, whose doubts defined his character.

While pessimism marked Thomas' doubts, Philip displayed doubts that sprang from rational considerations. Jesus was Joseph's son, how could He be divine (Jn 1:45)? We can't feed five thousand people because we don't have enough money among us to buy that much food (6:7). Sure we'd love to see the Father. Don't talk as though we've seen Him. Show Him to us (14:8). That's the way Philip's mind worked.

We face our doubts, too, perhaps when going away to college, struggling with the death of a loved one, or facing a health crisis. At times like these we find out what we really believe about God, what kind of relationship we really have with Him, and what we've accepted more or less superficially. At those times we have to struggle with doubt and unbelief until we internalize more biblical truth that will enable us to handle the new demands on our faith.

Philip found answers to his doubt and unbelief. Tradition tells us that after the coming of the Holy Spirit and the birth of the church, Philip spent the rest of his life preaching the good news in the provinces of Galatia and Phrygia in Asia Minor. We're also told that he died at Hierapolis, a city near Colosse and Laodicea

QUESTIONS FOR INTERACTION ─────────────

1. Philip needed evidence. He was a see-it-to-believe-it kind of guy. Which of these best describes how you process new ideas?
   a. I believe just about anything.
   b. I have an intuitive feel for what's true and what's false.
   c. Seeing and doing equal believing, not reading about something.
   d. I work through a series of logical steps to determine probability.
   e. I need proof before I believe even the clock or the calendar.

2. Philip raised objections at the feeding of the five thousand and in the upper room the night before Jesus died. How do you react to objection-raisers? How do you think you would have reacted to Philip's personality?

3. Where do you think Philip might have obtained all the information about Jesus that he gave Nathanael in John 1:45?

4. Why do you suppose Philip invited Nathanael to meet Jesus in light of his objections to Jesus being the Messiah (Jn 1:46)?

5. John wrote that Jesus asked Philip about buying bread to feed the 5,000 in order "to test him" (Jn 6:6). What might Jesus have wanted to find out about Philip?

6. What do you think Philip's answer to Jesus' question reveals about him and his understanding of Jesus (Jn 6:7)?

7. If you had been Philip, what would you have concluded about Jesus from the feeding of the 5,000? What would you have thought about the test Jesus put you through?

8. What does Philip's request for Jesus to show him the Father reveal about his understanding of the relationship between Jesus and the Father (Jn 14:8)?

9. What did Jesus expect His disciples to have concluded about His relation to the Father? On what bases should they have reached that conclusion (vv. 9-11)?

10. In what kinds of circumstances do you expect more evidence from God than He may want to give before you respond in faith to Him?

GOING DEEPER

11. When do you think it's good to be a little slow to believe, like Philip? How can that caution help you?

12. When do you think it's bad to be a slow to believe, like Philip? How can that caution harm you?

CARING TIME

People like Philip, who sincerely demand evidence before they believe, can become some of the most committed Christ-followers once their objections are answered. Don't be afraid to ask hard questions. Don't feel guilty for making spiritual teachers work hard to answer you. Just be sure you are humble and sincere in your search for the truth and in your obedience to the truth you discover.

1. What have you found to be some of the best sources of answers to your questions about the Bible and about Christianity?

2. How can we help our searching, unbelieving friends find answers to their intellectual objections to faith in Jesus?

3. What questions about your faith are you wrestling with presently that we can pray about with you?

NEXT WEEK

Next week we will look at the character of the apostle called Nathanael in the Gospel of John. He's the friend Philip brought to Jesus. The other Gospel writers call him Bartholomew. Nathanael Bartholomew displays a scrupulously religious personality. Sincerely confounded by Jesus, he had to get past some of his rigid traditionalism to receive the "new wine" of the gospel.

NOTES ON JOHN 1:35-39,43-49

1:37 two disciples. John identified Andrew as one of these disciples. The next day Philip told Nathanael, "We have found the One" (1:45). Philip makes the most likely candidate for Andrew's partner.

1:38 What are you looking for? Jesus wanted to know what motivated Andrew and Philip (2:24; 6:26).

1:39 Come and you'll see. Jesus invited Andrew and Philip to enter into the journey of discipleship with Him. Only as they committed themselves to follow Jesus would they perceive the nature of His true home and identity. ***10 in the morning.*** Various methods of reckoning time were used in the ancient world. John probably used a different method from the other three Gospels. If John had used the other method, the translation would be: "It was about 4 in the afternoon."

1:43 Galilee. Galilee, where Jesus was raised, was a province 60 miles north of Jerusalem. One of the reasons the Pharisees rejected Jesus' claim to messiahship was because they assumed He was born in Galilee (7:41, 52).

1:45 of whom Moses wrote in the law. This refers to the Prophet to come (Dt 18:18), the fulfillment of the Old Testament hope (Jn. 1:21).

1:46 Nazareth. This was a small, insignificant village in Galilee. It seemed

LESSON 5

impossible to Nathanael that the one Philip described could come from such a place. Besides, the Messiah was to be born in Bethlehem, the city of David (Mc 5:2).

NOTES ON JOHN 6:5-11

6:7 Two hundred denarii. A denarius was a full day's wage for a first-century laborer in Palestine. "Two hundred denarii worth of bread" represented a quantity of food that would require more than the wages from eight months of 6-day workweeks.

6:10 numbering about 5,000. According to Matthew 14:21 this number did not include women and children.

NOTES ON JOHN 14:1-11

14:1 Your heart must not be troubled. Having settled His own mind and heart, Jesus brought comfort to the disciples by giving them hope.

14:2 My Father's house. In 2:16 this referred to the temple. Here, it means heaven. The earthly temple was seen to be a symbol of the actual dwelling place of God (Heb 9:24). **many dwelling places.** The emphasis is not on having separate compartments in heaven, but on the abundance of room for all who will receive Jesus.

14:3 I will come back. This probably refers to the coming of Christ through His Spirit (vv. 15-21) rather than to the Second Coming, which receives very little attention in this Gospel. Through the Spirit, Jesus was "coming" to the disciples (v. 18), and they would then be "in" or "with" Him and the Father (vv. 20, 23). Seen in this way, this promise was not for the distant future, but would be true for the disciples in a very short time (20:22).

14:6 I am the way. The destination to which Jesus was going is not so much a place, but a person – the Father (7:33; 8:21). The way for the disciples to come to the Father was through the Son, who, by His death, opened the way for them (Heb 10:19-22).

14:11 believe because of the works themselves. The "signs" in chapters 1 – 12 were all given to point to the truth that Jesus came to reveal God's glory and bring life to people.

LESSON 5

NATHANAEL BARTHOLOMEW: SINCERELY CONFOUNDED

LAST WEEK

Last week we interacted with Philip, the pragmatic, rational apostle. We considered the importance of humility and sincerity in our intellectual searches for answers to tough spiritual questions. Philip modeled for us how to be open to truth while struggling with inherent skepticism. This week we turn to Nathanael Bartholomew, a friend of Philip. We'll see that this apostle possessed high moral principles that sometimes made him inflexible. Meeting Jesus confounded this sincere man.

ICE-BREAKER

Nathanael Bartholomew must have been a remarkably honest man. The first thing out of Jesus' mouth when He saw him was "Here is a true Israelite; no deceit is in him" (Jn 1:47). It would be an honor to be held in such high regard by the Son of God.

1. If the Lord Jesus were going to commend you for a character trait, which of these would you want Him to spotlight? Why?
   a. Integrity.
   b. Faith.
   c. Intelligence.
   d. Love.
   e. Holiness.
   f. Courage.
   g. Other _____.

2. When you were a boy, which of these labels did you probably wear in the minds of neighborhood adults? Why?
   a. The neighborhood bully.
   b. The neighborhood rule maker.
   c. The neighborhood salesman.
   d. The neighborhood Casanova.
   e. The neighborhood jock.
   f. The neighborhood crybaby.
   g. The neighborhood daredevil.
   h. Other _____.

BIBLICAL FOUNDATION

The apostle we look at this week bears a compound name. John, who wrote the most about him, called him Nathanael (Jn 1:45-51). The other Gospel writers identified him as Bartholomew (Mt 10:3; Mk 3:18; Lk 6:14). We'll call him Nathanael Bartholomew after the pattern of Simon Peter, who also had two names.

Essentially all we know about Nathanael Bartholomew we discover in his initial encounter with Jesus. Nathanael's friend Philip brought him to meet the One who seemed to fulfill the Old Testament messianic prophecies. Jesus looked into this man's heart and commended him for a dominant character trait. Then the Lord alluded to an Old Testament incident that forced Nathanael Bartholomew to change his opinion of this particular Nazarene.

A Scrupulously Honest Man

43 The next day He decided to leave for Galilee. Jesus found Philip and told him, "Follow Me!"44 Now Philip was from Bethsaida, the home-town of Andrew and Peter. 45 Philip found Nathanael and told him, "We have found the One Moses wrote about in the law (and so did the prophets): Jesus the son of Joseph, from Nazareth!" 46 "Can anything good come out of Nazareth?" Nathanael asked him. "Come and see," Philip answered. 47 Then Jesus saw Nathanael coming toward Him and said about him, "Here is a true Israelite; no deceit is in him." 48 "How do you know me?" Nathanael asked. "Before Philip called you, when you were under the fig tree, I saw you," Jesus answered. 49 "Rabbi," Nathanael replied, "You are the Son of God! You are the King of Israel!" 50 Jesus responded to him, "Do you believe [only] because I told you I saw you under the fig tree? You will see greater things than this." 51 Then He said, "I assure you: You will see heaven opened and the angels of God ascending and descending on the Son of Man."

John 1:43-51

The Way to God

10 Jacob left Beer-sheba and went toward Haran. 11 He reached a certain place and spent the night there because the sun had set. He took one of the stones from the place, put it there at his head, and lay down in that place. 12 And he dreamed: A stairway was set on the ground with its top reaching heaven, and God's angels were going up and down on it. 13 The Lord was standing there beside him, saying, "I am the Lord, the God of your father Abraham and the God of Isaac. . . . 15 Look, I am with you and will watch over you wherever you go. I will bring you back to this land, for I will not leave you until I have done what I have promised you."

16 When Jacob awoke from his sleep, he said, "Surely the Lord is in

this place, and I did not know it." [17] He was afraid and said, "What an awesome place this is! This is none other than the house of God. This is the gate of heaven."

Genesis 28:10-13a,15-17

Seeing the Risen Lord

[2] Simon Peter, Thomas (called "Twin"), Nathanael from Cana of Galilee, Zebedee's sons, and two others of His disciples were together. [3] "I'm going fishing," Simon Peter said to them. "We're coming with you," they told him. They went out and got into the boat, but that night they caught nothing. [4] When daybreak came, Jesus stood on the shore. However, the disciples did not know it was Jesus. [5] "Men," Jesus called to them, "you don't have any fish, do you?" "No," they answered. [6] "Cast the net on the right side of the boat," He told them, "and you'll find some." So they did, and they were unable to haul it in because of the large number of fish. [7] Therefore the disciple, the one Jesus loved, said to Peter, "It is the Lord!" When Simon Peter heard that it was the Lord, he tied his outer garment around him (for he was stripped) and plunged into the sea. [8] But since they were not far from land (about 100 yards away), the other disciples came in the boat, dragging the net full of fish. [9] When they got out on land, they saw a charcoal fire there, with fish lying on it, and bread. [10] "Bring some of the fish you've just caught," Jesus told them. [11] So Simon Peter got up and hauled the net ashore, full of large fish—153 of them. Even though there were so many, the net was not torn. [12] "Come and have breakfast," Jesus told them. None of the disciples dared ask Him, "Who are You?" because they knew it was the Lord. [13] Jesus came, took the bread, and gave it to them. He did the same with the fish. [14] This was now the third time Jesus appeared to the disciples after He was raised from the dead.

John 21:2-14

PRINCIPLE DEVELOPMENT

It should surprise no one that pragmatic Philip sought the opinion of a friend who also applied stringent criteria when assessing important situations. While Philip used logical tests on problems, Nathanael Bartholomew applied moral standards. He wanted to know how Jesus measured up to the righteous requirements of God's Law.

Jesus challenged Nathanael Bartholomew's limited understanding of righteousness in two ways. First, the Lord wanted him to realize that true righteousness is a matter of the heart rather than outward conformity to legal standards. Second, He wanted His newest follower to recognize that access to God comes only through an intimate relationship with Him. He is the "gate of heaven" (Gn 28:17; see Jn 1:51).

PRINCIPLE 1

Nathanael was a God-fearing Jew. He was scrupulously honest. Unfortunately he relied on his own good works and self-righteousness to earn eternal life. In this, Nathanael was dangerously wrong.

To Nathanael's credit, when he discovered that the only way to heaven was to put his faith in Jesus Christ, the Son of God, he did so. When he took this step, Nathanael experienced the transforming work of the Holy Spirit in his life that he could never have achieved through his own efforts. Nathanael came to realize that even his ancestor Abraham had been saved by faith. Paul expressed this point to the Roman Christians when he wrote:

"This is why the promise is by faith, so that it may be according to grace, to guarantee it to all [Abraham's] descendants – not only to those who are of the law, but also to those who are of Abraham's faith. He is the father of us all" (Rm 4:16).

PRINCIPLE 2

Nathanael was impressed with Jacob's experience at Bethel. God had revealed His greatness and holiness to this Old Testament scoundrel in a dream. When he woke, he could only whisper, "Surely the Lord is in this place, and I did not know it" (Gn 28:16).

When Jacob caught a glimpse of God's greatness and holiness, he recognized his own sinful condition. He saw himself as a deceiver and a manipulator. I believe he experienced justification by faith that night at Bethel.

Though Nathanael was an honest man, he, too, discovered he needed a Savior. Even though he was not a deceiver and manipulator like Jacob, he was still among those who "fall short of the glory of God" (Rm 3:23). Furthermore, his own self-righteousness could not earn him a place in heaven.

LESSON 6

PRINCIPLE 3

RECOGNIZING AND RECEIVING THE LORD JESUS CHRIST AS PERSONAL
SAVIOR FROM SIN IS THE ONLY WAY TO INHERIT ETERNAL LIFE.

When God revealed Himself in a dream at Bethel, Jacob saw a "stairway . .
. reaching heaven, and God's angels were going up and down on it" (Gn
28:12). Jesus alluded to this incident as He promised Nathanael
Bartholomew that he would see great miracles in the future (Jn 1:50-51).
On the evening before His crucifixion, Jesus told Nathanael Bartholomew
and the other apostles, "I am the way, the truth, and the life. No one comes
to the Father except through Me" (14:6). Within a few days Nathanael
Bartholomew, from Cana in Galilee (21:2), would be ready to spend the
rest of his life pointing to Jesus of Nazareth as the only way to God.

We, too, must face the question of Jesus' claims about Himself. Have
you received the Lord Jesus, the Son of God, as your personal Savior
from sin? He is the only way to God.

QUESTIONS FOR INTERACTION

1. What region of the country do you tend to look down on as back-
   ward or out-of-touch? How hard would it be for you to accept spiritual leadership from someone from there?

2. Philip thought that once Nathanael met Jesus he would forget his
   objection based on geography and prophecy (Jn 1:46). What could
   Nathanael learn about Jesus from a direct encounter that he could
   not learn by studying Him from a distance?

3. Do you think Nathanael was being immodest or frank when he casu-
   ally accepted Jesus' assessment that he was an exceptionally honest
   man (Jn 1:47-48a)? Why?

4. Why do you suppose Jesus' demonstration of supernatural vision convinced Nathanael to call Him "Rabbi," "Son of God," and "King of
   Israel" (Jn 1:49)?

5. What conclusions did Jacob draw about Bethel from the vision of
   angels ascending and descending the stairway (Gn 28:16-17)?

6. What claims was Jesus making about Himself by telling Nathanael
   "You will see heaven opened and the angels of God ascending and
   descending upon the Son of Man" (Jn 1:51)?

7. Many think Nathanael was meditating on Jacob's encounter with God at Bethel (Gn 28:10-17) while he sat under the fig tree (Jn 1:50). How would that have increased the impression Jesus' statements made on Nathanael (Jn 1:51)?
8. If you had been Nathanael Bartholomew in the fishing boat, when would you have known it was the resurrected Jesus on the shore (Jn 21:2-14)?

9. How would you have felt when the Lord, who knew you perfectly, rescued your failed fishing trip and then fixed you a warm breakfast?

GOING DEEPER

10. How did you come to realize that Jesus was the only way to get to God? Before that, what had you thought you needed to do to earn God's approval?

11. What do you find surprising about the fact that God wants to have an intimate relationship with you that involves talking with you and listening to your concerns and dreams?

CARING TIME

Nathanael Bartholomew needed to become less rigid and legalistic in his understanding of how God relates to people through Jesus Christ. He became more relational and more intimate in his concept of salvation and discipleship.

1. Do you tend to be naturally rule-oriented or relational in your approach to knowing God? How does that affect your feelings of intimacy with Him?
2. How can we help one another in this group grow in personal intimacy with God?
3. How can we involve men who haven't crossed the line of faith in our group so they can come to know Jesus?

NEXT WEEK

Next week we turn our attention to Matthew, the entrepreneur in the ranks of the apostles. Matthew represented a group of wealthy outcasts whom Jesus wanted to reach. His conversion and discipleship opened doors into a needy group many loved to hate.

1:46 Nazareth. This was a small, insignificant village in Galilee. It seemed impossible to Nathanael that the one Philip described could come from such a place. Besides, the Messiah was to be born in Bethlehem, the city of David (Mc 5:2).

1:47 a true Israelite. Nathanael, unlike Israel as a whole, came to Him with sincerity. Israel was supposed to be a people prepared to respond to God, but for the most part the nation failed to reflect that purpose.

1:48 I saw you. This accents Jesus' supernatural knowledge. Nathanael responded positively to Jesus' divine insight and personal interest directed at him.

1:50 greater things. This is probably an allusion to the miracles Jesus would perform as signs of His divine identity, culminated by the grand miracle of His resurrection.

1:51 This verse recalls Jacob's dream (Gn 28:10-22), with the significant difference that Jesus replaced the stairway as the means of communication between heaven and earth. The new Bethel (house of God – Gn 28:19) is found in Jesus Himself. ***the Son of Man.*** Of all the titles applied to Jesus in this chapter, this is the one He used for Himself. Daniel 7:13ff provides its background as the One invested with divine authority to rule the earth, but it was not a commonly-used term for the Messiah in Jesus' time.

NOTES ON GENESIS 28:10-17

28:11 He took one of the stones from the place, put it there at his head. As strange as it sounds, this made a more comfortable bed for Jacob. People traveled only with a cloak and some food, using the hard ground for a bed.

28:12 stairway. We may sing about "Jacob's ladder," but he probably saw a stairway. ***God's angels. . . on it.*** In this dream, God demonstrated that He wanted a relationship with Jacob, that He wanted to be not only the God of his grandfather Abraham and of his father Isaac, but of Jacob as well.

28:13 beside him. The Lord had come down to Jacob on the stairway. He showed Himself to be personal and relational, unlike the pagan gods. He invited Jacob into a relationship with Him.

28:15 I am with you. God had made this promise to Isaac (26:3). Again God promises to protect and sustain with His presence. ***I will not leave you.*** It did not matter where Jacob went, the one true God would be with him. Jacob was running away from all that he knew, but he could not run from what God had planned for him.

28:17 house of God. Jacob had experienced the God that his father had known (27:20). God Himself and His heaven had come down to the place where Jacob slept. Jacob was rightly in awe.

NOTES ON JOHN 21:2-14

21:2 Cana of Galilee. Cana lay about 8 miles northeast of Nazareth. Neither was an important place. Jesus performed His first miracle in Cana by turning water to wine at a wedding (2:1-11). Nathanael's initial contempt for Nazareth as Jesus' hometown (1:46) may have been triggered by a sense of the insignificance of the whole region.

21:7 the disciple whom Jesus loved. This is thought to be John, the author of the Gospel. ***It's the Lord!*** As Jesus' voice opened Mary's eyes to recognize Him (20:16), so here the enormous catch of fish revealed to the beloved disciple that the One to whom they were talking was the Lord.

21:12 breakfast. The Jesus they met was no disembodied spirit. They could see Him and hear Him and eat with Him. He had hands and feet that allowed Him to kindle a fire on the beach. Jesus had been resurrected bodily. He had conquered death.

21:14 the third time. This is the third resurrection account described in John's Gospel (20:19-23, 24-29). The post-resurrection appearances are important for a number of reasons. For one thing, they are part of the proof of Jesus' resurrection (along with the fact of the empty tomb, the collapsed and empty grave clothes, etc.). Second, they show that Jesus had conquered death. He was not simply a disembodied spirit who appeared as a ghost-like figure, a hallucination, or a vision. Third, they describe how it was that the disciples learned of their mission. Fourth, it was the encounter with the living Jesus that changed the disciples from frightened men in hiding to bold witnesses who changed the world. Finally, the post-resurrection appearances show to all of us that Jesus is still alive and thus we can enter into a personal relationship with Him even today.

LESSON 6

MATTHEW: ETERNAL ENTREPRENEUR

LAST WEEK

Last week we got acquainted with Nathanael Bartholomew, the man of integrity who was confounded when Jesus did not have a rules-oriented approach to spirituality. On their first encounter, Jesus commended him for being "a true Israelite; no deceit is in him" (Jn 1:47). It's almost easy to imagine Jesus wanting this man to be an apostle. This week we turn our attention to Matthew, about whose integrity Jesus could pay no compliments. Matthew was a wealthy man in a corrupt profession. He extorted taxes. It can be hard for us to imagine Jesus wanting this man as an apostle.

ICE-BREAKER

Some people are good at making money. They have the charisma and drive to make the sale or to close the deal. Matthew was the apostle who grew up to be a highly motivated entrepreneur who accumulated wealth. But he was a dishonest businessman. His ethics violated truth and honesty. His scruples went unheeded by his deadened conscience. Roman tax gatherers bid for the right to collect taxes in a district. Then they extorted by threat and force the set tax rate, the amount they bid for the job, and the profit they felt entitled to. Roman law enforcement and judiciary looked the other way.

1. When you were a boy, what did you really enjoy doing to make money? What did you really dislike doing that you had to do to make money?

2. Which of these characters are you most like when it comes to making money? Why?
   a. Eric the Entrepreneur – a million ideas to get rich.
   b. Irving the Investor – making my money work for me.
   c. Gary the Gambler – counting on the lottery.
   d. Larry the Laborer – hard work pays off.
   e. Jerry the Jinx – every deal goes sour.
   f. Charlie the Churchmouse – pinching pennies.
   g. Barry the Borrower – counting on making more tomorrow.
   h. Other _____.

Matthew was another apostle with two names, but one of them dropped away. When he first appeared in Mark and Luke (Mk 2:14; Lk 5:27), this tax collector went by Levi, the name of Jacob's son whose descendants served as priests in Israel. By the time Levi was an apostle, everyone called him Matthew (Mt 10:3; Mk 3:18; Lk 6:15).

In his own Gospel, Matthew always referred to himself as Matthew, never as Levi. He did not, however, hide his past. In the list of apostles, Matthew alone identified himself as "Matthew the tax collector" (10:3). Mark identified Matthew as "the son of Alphaeus" (Mk 2:14). The other James among the apostles, whom we'll consider in lesson 9, was also "the son of Alphaeus" (Mt 10:3; Mk 3:18; Lk 6:15). The Gospel writers all group Matthew with Thomas in their lists of apostles. None suggests that Matthew and James were brothers, even though their fathers bore the same name.

An Apostle to the Up-and-Out

[27] After this, Jesus went out and saw a tax collector named Levi sitting at the tax office, and He said to him, "Follow Me!" [28] So, leaving everything behind, he got up and began to follow Him. [29] Then Levi hosted a grand banquet for Him at his house. Now there was a large crowd of tax collectors and others who were guests with them. [30] But the Pharisees and their scribes were complaining to His disciples, "Why do you eat and drink with tax collectors and sinners?"

[31] Jesus replied to them, "The healthy don't need a doctor, but the sick do. [32] I have not come to call the righteous, but sinners to repentance."

Luke 5:27-31

[9] As Jesus went on from there, He saw a man named Matthew sitting at the tax office, and He said to him, "Follow Me!" So he got up and followed Him. [10] While He was reclining at the table in the house, many tax collectors and sinners came as guests to eat with Jesus and His disciples. [11] When the Pharisees saw this, they asked His disciples, "Why does your Teacher eat with tax collectors and sinners?" [12] But when He heard this, He said, "Those who are well don't need a doctor, but the sick do. [13] Go and learn what this means: I desire mercy and not sacrifice. For I didn't come to call the righteous, but sinners."

Matthew 9:9-13

Faith and Money Don't Mix

[13] [Jesus taught His disciples,] "No servant can be the slave of two mas-

ters, since either he will hate one and love the other, or he will be devoted to one and despise the other. You can't be slaves to both God and money." ¹⁴ The Pharisees, who were lovers of money, were listening to all these things and scoffing at Him. ¹⁵ And He told them: "You are the ones who justify yourselves in the sight of others, but God knows your hearts. For what is highly admired by people is revolting in God's sight."

Luke 16:13-15

¹⁸ A ruler asked Him, "Good Teacher, what must I do to inherit eternal life?" ¹⁹ "Why do you call Me good?" Jesus asked him. "No one is good but One—God. ²⁰ You know the commandments:

Do not commit adultery; do not murder; do not steal; do not bear false witness; honor your father and mother."

²¹ "I have kept all these from my youth," he said.

²² When Jesus heard this, He told him, "You still lack one thing: sell all that you have and distribute it to the poor, and you will have treasure in heaven. Then come, follow Me."

²³ After he heard this, he became extremely sad, because he was very rich.

²⁴ Seeing that he became sad, Jesus said, "How hard it is for those who have wealth to enter the kingdom of God! ²⁵ For it is easier for a camel to go through the eye of a needle than for a rich person to enter the kingdom of God." ²⁶ Those who heard this asked, "Then who can be saved?" ²⁷ He replied, "What is impossible with men is possible with God."

Luke 18:18-27

PRINCIPLE DEVELOPMENT

We can learn a lot from Matthew, even though we thankfully may not be able to identify with the extent of his dishonesty and greed. We all face the challenge to put Jesus Christ at the center of our lives. Ask the Holy Spirit to help you apply the lessons we can learn from this first-century materialist who became a dynamic witness for the Lord.

PRINCIPLE 1

JESUS CHRIST WANTS ALL CHRISTIANS TO SEEK FIRST HIS KINGDOM AND HIS RIGHTEOUSNESS.

Matthew had built his life around money and power. He swore allegiance to Rome, the hated world power of his day, in order to oppress his fellow countrymen for personal gain. For Matthew to turn his eyes toward righteousness and the kingdom of God required a shift of values that few men ever have to make to be Christ-followers.

Matthew probably didn't realize the full implications of his initial decision to abandon tax collecting in favor of following Jesus. Certainly he knew he would lose his income for the time he followed the Master. Eventually, he realized there was no going back. To follow Jesus precluded greed and graft.

John the Baptist told tax collectors, "Don't collect any more than what you have been authorized" (Lk 3:13). Tax collecting could be done honorably, but Matthew had a calling to spread the gospel to all nations (Mt 28:19-20). For him, putting God's kingdom and righteousness first involved fulltime ministry. For you it may involve professional ministry, or it may involve building the kingdom with your time or wealth as a layperson.

PRINCIPLE 2

JESUS CHRIST IS STILL LOOKING FOR MEN OF MEANS WHO WILL FAITHFULLY USE THEIR RESOURCES TO BUILD THE KINGDOM OF GOD.

The first thing Matthew did as a new disciple was gather all his tax collector friends at a banquet so they could learn about Jesus, too (Lk 5:29). Zacchaeus, a chief tax collector who later came to faith in Jesus, distributed half his possessions among the poor and offered to pay quadruple restitution to anyone he had overcharged (19:8). There were potential disciples among Matthew's cronies.

In the Sermon on the Mount, Jesus taught His disciples, "Don't collect for yourselves treasures on earth, where moth and rust destroy and where thieves break in and steal. But collect for yourselves treasures in heaven, where neither moth nor rust destroys, and where thieves don't break in and steal. For where your treasure is, there your heart will be also" (Mt 6:19-21).

Matthew is the Gospel writer who best remembered Jesus' teaching about financial resources in relationship to the kingdom of God. He best understood what it meant to invest everything where it would pay eternal dividends.

PRINCIPLE 3

JESUS CHRIST WANTS GENEROUS CHRISTIAN BUSINESSMEN TO BECOME MODELS AND EXAMPLES TO OTHER BUSINESSMEN WHO IN TURN WILL BECOME GENEROUS BUSINESSMEN.

God used Matthew, a transformed materialist, to help us understand the "gospel of giving." Entrepreneurs who decide to use their resources to the full to build the kingdom of God are great models. We need these examples.

Someone might quote Jesus' statement, "But when you give to the poor, don't let your left hand know what your right hand is doing, so that your giving may be in secret. And your Father who sees in secret will reward you" (Mt 6:3-4). Jesus aimed His warning at the Pharisees who gave for the purpose of being seen, admired, and applauded. Anyone whose philanthropy is motivated by applause needs to heed Jesus' warning. Everyone who gives to meet needs and stimulate the growth of God's kingdom needs to be noted by the church, as Barnabas was (Ac 4:36-37). Other believers are encouraged in their hearts and are stimulated to imitate such good examples.

QUESTIONS FOR INTERACTION

1. When you think of Matthew making the transition from tax collector to disciple, do you consider his experience with wealth an asset or a liability in learning to follow Jesus? Why?

2. Which of these is the greatest discipleship issue that money poses for you?
   a. I don't earn enough to consider tithing.
   b. I can't decide whether I live too extravagantly.
   c. My wife and I can't agree on how much to give.
   d. I vacillate between doing more for the kingdom and working to earn more money.
   e. I think I like material possessions too much.
   f. I'm inclined to give too much away.
   g. Other _____.

3. How did each of these feel about the "grand banquet" (Lk 5:29) for all the tax collectors? Matthew? The Pharisees and scribes? Jesus?

4. In Jesus' opinion, what was wrong with the attitude of the Pharisees and scribes toward His associating with the tax collectors (Mt 9:11-13; Lk 5:30-31)?

5. Why, according to Jesus, does money make a bad master (Lk 16:13-15)?

6. What was wrong with the Pharisees' philosophy about money (Lk 16:14-15)?

7. Why do you suppose Jesus let the rich young ruler affirm his moral accomplishments before He pointed out his crucial moral defect (Lk 18:19-21)?

8. Why do you think Jesus demanded that the rich young ruler sell everything he had and give the proceeds to the poor (Lk 16:22)?

9. According to Jesus, what is the special difficulty for a wealthy person concerning entering the kingdom of God (Lk 18:24-27)?

10. How can you use your money and your possessions to advance the kingdom of God?

GOING DEEPER

11. How do your possessions try to own you?

12. How can your experiences (good and bad) with money make you a more effective witness for Christ?

CARING TIME

Matthew's initial ministry grew out of his background in finance. He had contacts with money people that none of the other apostles could have. He reached out to his friends and former associates. No doubt Matthew's transformed values and lifestyle prepared the way for Jesus' teaching in the hearts and lives of the assembled tax collectors.

1. What kind of people have your experiences with money prepared you to understand and empathize with?

2. How would you like your attitude toward money and possessions to change? How can this group help you with that?

3. How can we support you in prayer concerning your use of your possessions to advance the kingdom of God?

NEXT WEEK

Next week we shift from studying a materialist to examining a pessimist. Thomas possessed the temperament of a stubborn naysayer. It seems that most groups have a member who sees every glass as half empty. The Lord

Jesus, however, was not content to leave Thomas' pessimism alone. He challenged Thomas to concentrate his heart and soul on positive belief and action.

NOTES ON LUKE 5:27-31

5:28 Levi. A former name for Matthew (Mt 9:9). Both names are Hebrew. Levi meant, "Joined." Matthew meant, "Gift of the Lord."

5:29 a grand banquet. Luke includes a number of banquets or feasts. Some are earthly celebrations; others look towards a heavenly meal (7:36-50; 9:10-17; 10:38-42; 11:37-54; 14:1-24; 15:23; 22:16-18; 23:43; 24:28-32, 41-43. *tax collectors.* Considered as vile as robbers and murderers, these Jews were seen as traitors because they collaborated with the Roman power to become wealthy. Since only the tax collectors knew the tax rate required by Rome, they charged whatever the market would bear. Once they paid what they owed Rome, they could keep the rest.

5:30 Why do you eat? To eat with someone was to accept that person. The Pharisees could not understand how a truly righteous person could eat with people whose moral lives were disreputable and who ate food that was prepared and served in ways that violated the practices regarding ritual cleanliness.

NOTES ON MATTHEW 9:9-13

9:9 Matthew. The author of this Gospel. In his role as tax collector, Matthew would have been hated by both the religious establishment and the common people. *the tax office.* Matthew's toll booth probably sat on the northern end of the Sea of Galilee near the Syrian border and on a heavily traveled trade route that came from Damascus. If so, Matthew collected taxes on both imports and exports. *Follow Me!* In Matthew, Mark, and Luke, this is the key phrase regarding discipleship. Only those who leave their past behind to follow Jesus in faith and obedience are His disciples.

9:12 Those who are well don't need a doctor, but the sick do. Jesus was not necessarily saying that the Pharisees were spiritually healthy, only that they perceived themselves to be so.

9:13 I desire mercy and not sacrifice. This quotation from Hosea 6:6 sheds light on how Jesus would go about healing the "sick" to whom He had been sent – through mercy, not through requiring more observance of religious ritual.

18:18 ruler. Perhaps this person was a leader of a synagogue (like Jairus – 8:41) or even a member of the Sanhedrin, the official Jewish ruling council. **what must I do?** The emphasis on gaining the kingdom by virtue of one's religious activities stands in sharp contrast to Jesus' teaching about receiving the kingdom by faith (18:16-17).

18:20 the commandments. Jesus cited five of the Ten Commandments, those that deal with a person's relationship toward others (Ex 20:12-16). Significantly, He omitted both the first ("Do not have other gods besides Me") and the tenth ("Do not covet"). Those are the commandments that later proved to be the stumbling blocks for this ruler.

18:22 You still lack one thing. Jesus did not refute the man's claim to be obedient to the demands of the commandments, but He pointed out that this had not touched his inner attitude of love for God or his neighbor. **sell all that you have.** Jesus used this command to show the ruler that wealth was his true god and his self-centered use of his money his true love. Jesus was not saying with this teaching that all people who seek eternal life must sell all their possessions. He was saying, give full allegiance to the true God. **follow Me.** The ultimate demand of the kingdom is for absolute allegiance to Jesus over one's self and possessions (16:13). This the ruler did not accept.

18:24 How hard it is. Jesus contradicted the common assumption that wealth is the verification that one had led a godly life (Jb 1:10; Ps 128:1-2). Instead, wealth is actually a barrier that can prevent people from seeing their need for God.

LESSON 7

Thomas: A Wounded Witness

Last Week

Last week we ran into Matthew, the first of the apostles whose background was decidedly shady. Somewhere in his past, Matthew had decided to abandon everything his culture held dear, pledge allegiance to the Roman occupiers, and make a killing by extorting taxes from his fellow countrymen. This entrepreneur had to abandon the worship of money to follow Jesus. He's an interesting case study for men living today in the most materialistic civilization of all time.

This week our subject is Thomas. Try as he might, Thomas had serious doubts. Eventually this included Jesus. However, his crisis of doubt turned into the moment when his faith burst out triumphantly.

Ice-Breaker

Thomas and Philip appear together before and after the crucifixion, resurrection, and ascension of Jesus (Jn 14:5-8; Ac 1:13). Perhaps their pessimism drew them together in stressful times. In the Gospel apostolic lists, Thomas is paired with Matthew (Mt 10:3; Mk 3:18; Lk 6:15). Maybe Matthew looked on the brighter side of things and cheered his gloomier colleague.

1. If you wake up in the middle of the night to hear wind howling and rain lashing your house, which of these is your default reaction?
   a. The basement's going to leak, and a tree will blow over on the house.
   b. Rain! Rats! I'll get wet going to work.
   c. I'm glad I'm in my warm bed and not out in that!
   d. Wow, it's been a while since we've had a storm this bad. Keep us safe, Lord.
   e. Oh boy! I love nasty weather. I want to get up and watch the show.

2. Are you more like your mother or your father in your pessimism/optimism? In what ways are you like this parent?

BIBLICAL FOUNDATION

Thomas is the English version of a Hebrew name that means "Twin." In John's Gospel Thomas is identified as "Thomas (called 'Twin')" (11:16; 21:2). The second name, translated "Twin," is the Greek term "Didymus." Did Thomas have a twin brother or sister? Maybe. On the other hand, Thomas could have been a family name handed down from generation to generation.

The Gospels reveal nothing of Thomas' background or occupation. He went fishing in Galilee with six other apostles between the resurrection and ascension of Jesus (Jn 21:2). Thomas is not mentioned by name after the first chapter of Acts.

Grimly Determined

¹ Now a man was sick, Lazarus, from Bethany, the village of Mary and her sister Martha. . . . ³ So the sisters sent a message to Him: "Lord, the one You love is sick." . . . ⁶ So when He heard that he was sick, He stayed two more days in the place where He was. ⁷ Then after that, He said to the disciples, "Let's go to Judea again." ⁸ "Rabbi," the disciples told Him, "just now the Jews tried to stone You, and You're going there again?" . . .¹⁴ So Jesus then told them plainly, "Lazarus has died. ¹⁵ I'm glad for you that I wasn't there so that you may believe. But let's go to him." ¹⁶ Then Thomas (called "Twin") said to his fellow disciples, "Let's go so that we may die with Him."

John 11:1, 3, 6-8, 14-16

Stubbornly Confused

1 "Your heart must not be troubled. Believe in God; believe also in Me. ² In My Father's house are many dwelling places; if not, I would have told you. I am going away to prepare a place for you. ³ If I go away and prepare a place for you, I will come back and receive you to Myself, so that where I am you may be also. ⁴ You know the way where I am going." ⁵ "Lord," Thomas said, "we don't know where You're going. How can we know the way?" ⁶ Jesus told him, "I am the way, the truth, and the life. No one comes to the Father except through Me. ⁷ "If you know Me, you will also know My Father. From now on you do know Him and have seen Him."

John 14:1-7

Bordering on Unbelief

24 But one of the Twelve, Thomas (called "Twin"), was not with them when Jesus came. 25 So the other disciples kept telling him, "We have

seen the Lord!" But he said to them, "If I don't see the mark of the nails in His hands, put my finger into the mark of the nails, and put my hand into His side, I will never believe!" ²⁶ After eight days His disciples were indoors again, and Thomas was with them. Even though the doors were locked, Jesus came and stood among them. He said, "Peace to you!" ²⁷ Then He said to Thomas, "Put your finger here and observe My hands. Reach out your hand and put it into My side. Don't be an unbeliever, but a believer." ²⁸ Thomas responded to Him, "My Lord and my God!" ²⁹ Jesus said, "Because you have seen Me, you have believed. Those who believe without seeing are blessed."

John 20:24-29

PRINCIPLE DEVELOPMENT

Tradition says Thomas became a great missionary in India, where he established the church and died a martyr. Supposedly, he fell mortally wounded by a spear. If so, it was rather an ironic way to die for the man who demanded to thrust his hand into the spear wound in Jesus' side. Perhaps Thomas was named "Twin" to indicate the Holy Spirit wants to speak through his example to those who are spiritually his "twin," men who tend to be pessimistic about life's situations?

PRINCIPLE I

IT'S POSSIBLE TO BE A PESSIMISTIC PERSONALITY YET A SINCERE FOL-LOWER OF JESUS CHRIST.

All of us have basic tendencies that drive us and motivate us to react in certain ways. Some of these traits are innate. They form the basic pattern we're born with. Some of these traits are also developed in our environment. But whatever the source, it is important to understand that the Holy Spirit wants to transform us into the image of Jesus Christ. Though Thomas was the kind of man who was affected by both his heredity and environment, he was still a very sincere follower of Jesus Christ. He asserted his willingness to die for the Lord before any of the other apostles (Jn 11:16). Even so, he battled pessimism. He allowed the realities of life to move him in the direction of being skeptical, negative, and untrusting. Consequently, his communication style often reflected sarcasm, arrogance, and a critical spirit. Furthermore, Thomas often put his faith in his own abilities, which also made him hesitant to trust others. As a result, he had difficulty understanding and accepting the supernatural dimensions of life.

In spite of his pessimistic approach to life, Thomas brings us a message of hope. Though we'll never change the basic pattern with which we were born, we can change the way we respond to the circumstances in our lives. We can learn to reflect the fruit of the Holy Spirit.

PRINCIPLE 2

IT'S POSSIBLE TO BE A VERY LOGICAL AND RATIONAL THINKER YET BE SPIRITUALLY CONFUSED.

Though Thomas could function in a very logical and rational way, he didn't understand who Jesus really was. He was spiritually confused. Just so, you may be a clear thinker from a human point of view. Yet you may have some unique blind spots spiritually and theologically. Unfortunately, you may not even recognize that this is true.

I personally believe that Thomas began to experience spiritual discernment the day he questioned Jesus about the way to the Father (Jn 14:5). At that moment, the Holy Spirit revealed to him who Jesus really was. Spiritual truth is spiritually discerned. Without supernatural assistance, Thomas would have remained confused.

Though he still entered a period of doubt and continued to battle his pessimistic tendencies, Thomas had become a new creation in Christ Jesus. By the end of the Gospel of John he had moved from being a carnal, worldly Christian to being a man controlled and directed by the Holy Spirit.

PRINCIPLE 3

IT'S POSSIBLE FOR A TRUE BELIEVER TO EXPERIENCE A CRISIS OF FAITH THAT CREATES A COMPLETE STATE OF DOUBT.

Thomas was not with the other apostles when Jesus made His first post-resurrection appearance. Perhaps he was so angry, wounded, and disillusioned that he simply went off by himself to regain perspective. It would make sense that he would try to revert to his old ways of doing things: trying to cope at a rational level.

Thomas did not permanently disassociate himself from the other apostles. He reappeared only to hear he had missed out on an incredible experience. Thomas immediately put up his mental and emotional guard. He would not risk reopening his wound. He would not trust the report that his fellow disciples gave him.

Seven days later, Jesus once again appeared, calmed the fears of His apostles, and turned to face Thomas. He invited His doubting disciple to put his fingers and his hands into the wounds that were still visible. He then told Thomas, "Don't be an unbeliever, but a believer" (Jn 20:27). Thomas processed his answer to Jesus' challenge in a split second. He knew this was another miracle that demonstrated Jesus Christ was who He claimed to be. He exclaimed with joy: "My Lord and my God!" (v. 28). His rebound was immediate and comprehensive.

QUESTIONS FOR INTERACTION

1. Do you react positively or negatively to skeptical people like Thomas? Why?

2. How would you like your outlook on life to become more balanced on the continuum between optimism and pessimism?

3. When Jesus wanted to go tend to Lazarus, Thomas said, "Let's go so that we may die with Him." What's the best explanation you can give for Thomas' response? The worst?

4. Thomas was the first apostle to express willingness to be wounded and die with Jesus. Why do you think he said it to the other apostles rather than to Jesus?

5. Thomas told Jesus that he and the other apostles did not know where Jesus was going or how to get there (Jn 14:5). How do you imagine the other apostles felt about Thomas' statement? How do you suppose Jesus felt about it?

6. Why do you think Jesus gave Thomas more evidence of His resurrection than He gave the other apostles (Jn 20:27-29)?

7. What was Thomas asserting when he called Jesus "my Lord and my God" (Jn 20:28)?

8. What do you think is the blessing of embracing what the Bible tells us about who Jesus is, without demanding empirical evidence as a prerequisite (Jn 20:29)?

9. In what area(s) of life do doubts interfere with your spiritual growth?

10. How can focusing on Jesus as the way, the truth, and the life diminish your doubts and increase your faith so you can progress spiritually?

GOING DEEPER

11. Do you find that rational thought and study clarify the Christian faith for you or confuse it? Why do you think that is?

12. Spiritual truth must be spiritually discerned. What is the role of the Holy Spirit in illuminating our minds to understand the Christian faith?

13. What life crises have created doubts for you about your faith? How did you recover from them?

CARING TIME

Jesus was patient with Thomas' doubts and generous in the way He provided answers to those doubts. We, too, should be patient with others who doubt. We should not despair of the Lord's patience when our own stubborn doubts cause us to disappoint Him.

1. Would you like to be more optimistic about life or more critical in your thinking? How can this group help you do that?

2. What doubt or life crisis is troubling you presently? How can we pray for you?

3. How can we encourage other men to "fill the empty chair" in our group?

NEXT WEEK

Next week we look at three seldom-noticed apostles. We know next-to-nothing about them. Whereas Thomas had a definite character, that of a doubter, James, Simon, and Judas must be considered generally. We will use them to explore the specific role the apostles played in spreading the gospel and founding the church. The Lord Jesus chose these men, whom we regard as anonymous, for their specific personalities, gifts, and passions. We may not know what they were, but the Lord did. He chose them, sent them out, and used them mightily.

11:6 He stayed two more days in the place where He was. At least two views are possible as to why He did this: (1) As in 2:3-4, Jesus seemingly ignored an urgent request to act in a needy situation. Jesus' delay communicated that His agenda is set neither by Himself (6:38) nor by the desires of those He loves, but by the Father. (2) He waited so that through this trial His glory would be revealed in a new way.

11:7 Let's go to Judea again. Jesus was in Perea on the other side of the Jordan River (10:40-42).

11:16 "Let's go so that we may die with Him." Although Thomas has become famous for his doubt (20:25), here he demonstrated his deep faith and loyalty, even though it also reflected his pessimistic nature.

NOTES ON JOHN 14:1-7

14:3 I will come back. This probably refers to the coming of Christ through His Spirit (vv. 16-21) rather than to the Second Coming, which receives very little attention in this Gospel. Through the Spirit, Jesus "returns" to the disciples (v. 18), and they are then "in" or "with" Him and the Father (vv. 20, 23). Seen in this way, this promise was not for the distant future, but would be true for the disciples in a very short time (20:22).

14:6 I am the way. The destination to which Jesus was going is not so much a place, but a person – the Father (7:33; 8:21). The way for the disciples to come to the Father was through the Son, who, by His death, opened the way for them (Heb 10:19-22).

NOTES ON JOHN 20:24-29

20:24 Thomas (called "Twin"). "Twin" translates the Greek noun "Didymus." The Hebrew name that becomes Thomas in English also meant "twin." **was not with them when Jesus came.** Thomas is often vilified because of the doubt he expressed in this story (v. 25). However, it needs to be asked what it says about Thomas that he was not with the other disciples at that time. Perhaps this indicates that Thomas was also a little less fearful than the others. In another context, it was Thomas who, when Jesus talked about going to Jerusalem to die, bravely asserted, "Let's go so that we may die with Him" (11:16).

20:26 Even though the doors were locked. This indicates that Jesus' resurrection was not limited in the way a normal physical body might be limited. He was able to enter a locked room and simply appear. Nevertheless His body could be felt (v. 27), and he ate (v. 19; Lk 24:41-43). **Peace.** A common Hebrew greeting (vv. 19, 21). The term reflects the salvation that Christ's redemptive work achieved: total well-being and inner rest of spirit in fellowship with God.

20:28 My Lord and my God! Thomas clearly affirmed the deity of Jesus. This is the last of a series of confessions of faith that sum up what John wanted the reader to recognize about Jesus (11:27).

20:29 Blessed are those who believe without seeing. John applied Jesus' words spoken to Thomas to the situation of his readers. They are not deprived because of never having seen Jesus. Indeed, He is with them through the Spirit (14:15-20) just as He was with the apostles.

James, Simon, and Judas: Unnoticed But Not Unrewarded

Last Week

Last week we met Thomas, the apostle with a decidedly pessimistic outlook on life. By nature he doubted situations and people, came across as sarcastic and arrogant, and tried the patience of his friends. Jesus met Thomas head on. He treated Thomas patiently but firmly. He led Thomas to move beyond self-protective doubting to a deep faith. This week we look at three apostles who are almost anonymous within the pages of Scripture. Our Lord Jesus saw them as chosen servants upon whom He planned to build His church. We may seldom notice them, but God would reward them.

Ice-Breaker

Back in the 1960s pop artist Andy Warhol claimed that, given the state of instant communication and electronic interconnectedness, everybody would enjoy at least fifteen minutes of fame in their lifetimes. It isn't so. Certainly a lot more people do enjoy minor celebrity status or notoriety for an instant before slipping back into anonymity. However, most people still live their lives below the radar beam of public awareness.

1. Which of these describes the highest level of fame you have enjoyed. Elaborate.
   a. National news.
   b. Local news.
   c. The school newspaper.
   d. The church bulletin.
   e. The school yearbook (without a picture).
   f. Other _____.

2. When you were young, in which of these areas did you imagine yourself excelling? Explain.
   a. Athletics.
   b. Entertainment.
   c. Medicine.
   d. Law.

e. Business.

f. Science.

g. The military.

h. Other _____.

BIBLICAL FOUNDATION

As you reach the end of the list of apostles, the names get less famil-iar. The men at the end of the list don't appear in the stories of the Gospels or the book of Acts. It may be tempting to discount them as unimportant figures who never did anything of consequence. However, tongues of fire rested on them at Pentecost, and they proclaimed the glo-ries of God. They form an integral part of the foundation on which the Holy Spirit is still building the church of Jesus Christ.

Faces in the Crowd

[13] Then He went up the mountain and summoned those He wanted, and they came to Him. [14] He appointed 12, whom He also named apostles, that they might be with Him and that He might send them out to preach [15] and to have authority to drive out demons.

Mark 3:13-15

[14] Simon, whom He also named Peter, and Andrew his brother; James and John; Philip and Bartholomew; [15] Matthew and Thomas; James the son of Alphaeus, and Simon called the Zealot; [16] Judas the son of James, and Judas Iscariot, who became a traitor.

Luke 6:14-16

Men on a Mission

[4] While He was together with them, He commanded them not to leave Jerusalem, but to wait for the Father's promise. . . .

[7] He said to them, "It is not for you to know times or periods that the Father has set by His own authority. [8] But you will receive power when the Holy Spirit has come upon you, and you will be My witnesses in Jerusalem, in all Judea and Samaria, and to the ends of the earth." . . .

[1] When the day of Pentecost had arrived, they were all together in one place. [2] Suddenly a sound like that of a violent rushing wind came from heaven, and it filled the whole house where they were staying.

[3] And tongues, like flames of fire that were divided, appeared to them and rested on each one of them. [4] Then they were all filled with the Holy Spirit and began to speak in different languages, as the Spirit gave them ability for speech.

LESSON 9

⁵ There were Jews living in Jerusalem, devout men from every nation under heaven. ⁶ When this sound occurred, the multitude came together and was confused because each one heard them speaking in his own language. ⁷ And they were astounded and amazed, saying, . . . "We hear them speaking in our own languages the magnificent acts of God."

Acts 1:4a, 7-8; 2:1-7a, 11b

Foundation of the Church

¹⁹ So then you are no longer foreigners and strangers, but fellow citizens with the saints, and members of God's household, ²⁰ built on the foundation of the apostles and prophets, with Christ Jesus Himself as the cornerstone. ²¹ The whole building is being fitted together in Him and is growing into a holy sanctuary in the Lord, ²² in whom you also are being built together for God's dwelling in the Spirit.

Ephesians 2:19-22

⁹ Then one of the seven angels, who had held the seven bowls filled with the seven last plagues, came and spoke with me: "Come, I will show you the bride, the wife of the Lamb." ¹⁰ He then carried me away in the Spirit to a great and high mountain and showed me the holy city, Jerusalem, coming down out of heaven from God, ¹¹ arrayed with God's glory. Her radiance was like a very precious stone, like a jasper stone, bright as crystal. ¹² [The city] had a massive high wall, with 12 gates. Twelve angels were at the gates; [on the gates], names were inscribed, the names of the 12 tribes of the sons of Israel. ¹³ There were three gates on the east, three gates on the north, three gates on the south, and three gates on the west. ¹⁴ The city wall had 12 foundations, and on them were the 12 names of the Lamb's 12 apostles.

Revelation 21:9-14

PRINCIPLE DEVELOPMENT

Jesus chose twelve men to help Him carry out the most significant task of all time: the establishment of His church on the earth. No head of state or CEO of a multinational corporation has ever born responsibility as important as that which each of the apostles carried. Their task transcends history. It's part of a plan God devised before time began, and what they accomplished will endure eternally when time is no more. Ironically, three of the twelve apostles survive in history as little more than names on a list. We know next to nothing about them and can conjecture little more. Their earthly fame parallels yours and mine. However, in God's eyes, they were giants.

PRINCIPLE 1

GOD WILL NOT FORGET WHAT WE DO TO BUILD HIS KINGDOM THOUGH FEW PEOPLE KNOW WHO WE ARE.

The writers of the Gospels and the book of Acts selected their material to make points and develop themes. Their accounts are not exhaustive records of the life of Jesus and the ministries of the apostles. Of the three apostles in this lesson, only Judas, son of James, made a cameo appearance in a Gospel narrative (Jn 14:22). Acts focused on Peter and Paul so intently, that virtually little is said of the ministries of all the other apostles except John. We don't know what James the son of Alphaeus, Simon the Zealot, and Judas the son of James did to extend the kingdom of God. We know from the book of Hebrews that "God is not unjust; He will not forget your work and the love you showed for His name when you served the saints" (6:10).

James, Simon, and Judas stand in the vanguard of the last who will be first (Mt 19:30), of those who have labored in anonymity on earth only to receive great reward in heaven (6:1-6), and of the poor in spirit to whom the kingdom of heaven belongs (5:3). Jesus saw qualities in them that made them men He wanted around Him. In eternity we, too, will fully appreciate their greatness.

PRINCIPLE 2

GOD WANTS TO USE OUR UNIQUE PERSONALITIES TO DO HIS KINGDOM WORK.

Of James, son of Alphaeus, we know next to nothing. He probably wasn't a forceful personality, but a behind-the-scenes laborer who willingly let others receive recognition. Simon the Zealot, on the other hand, probably was a fiery, cause-driven character. After all, the Zealots were political fanatics who later became the terrorist assassins known as Sicarii, the "Daggermen." How hard it must have been for Simon to learn to love his enemies and turn the other cheek.

Judas, son of James, may have preferred to go by Thaddaeus (Mt 10:3; Mk 3:18) in the days after Judas Iscariot betrayed Jesus. Thaddaeus roughly means "The Beloved." The King James Version, following some late Greek manuscripts, also refers to him as Lebbaeus, which means "Man of Heart." These names suggest that Judas, son of James, exhibited warmth and compassion.

No matter what our unique design and background, God has a special place for each of us in the body of Jesus Christ. True, He wants to mold all of us into His image so that we reflect the fruit of the Holy Spirit. At the same time He wants to use our uniqueness. He wanted what only James, Simon, and Judas could bring to the apostles then. He wants what only you can bring to His church today.

PRINCIPLE 3

NO MATTER WHAT PEOPLE CALL US, WHAT WE ARE IN OUR HEARTS IS WHAT COUNTS WITH GOD.

Sometimes a name change is in order. The apostles renamed Joseph and called him Barnabas, meaning "Son of encouragement" (Ac 4:36). Jesus changed Simon's name to Peter or Cephas to indicate his leadership role among the apostles (Jn 1:42). Saul's name was changed to Paul – perhaps to help him shed his image as a persecutor of Christians. Levi became Matthew, and Judas was called Thaddaeus. It seems all these names changes were made to give these men new identities.

People look at externals; God looks at our heart (1 Sm 16:7). What we are in our inner being is what counts with God. God does not evaluate our lives by the names, titles, accolades, or criticisms other people aim at us. He looks at our desire to serve Him and to walk in His will.

PRINCIPLE 4

THE MOST IMPORTANT RECOGNITION WE CAN EVER HAVE IS WHEN OUR NAMES APPEAR IN THE BOOK OF LIFE.

When all is said and done, the final chapter of history is written, and eternity begins, "many who are first will be last, and the last first" (Mt 19:30). Many people who are honored in this life will not be present in heaven. They will have had their reward on earth and will spend eternity separated from Jesus Christ because they did not receive the free gift of salvation that He offered them (Eph 2:8-9).

The apostles led the way and have their names on the foundation of the New Jerusalem (Rv 21:14). To join them there in eternity, we must receive Jesus Christ as Savior so that our names appear in the Book of Life (20:12,15). Then our eternal abode will be with the Lord and His apostles throughout eternity.

QUESTIONS FOR INTERACTION

1. Are you surprised, puzzled, disappointed, or encouraged that there are apostles about whom we know very little? Why?

2. Which of these best captures your opinion about the recognition you receive in your employment?
   a. I do the work, and someone else gets the credit.
   b. It's no fun being in the public eye. I wish I were more anonymous.
   c. I love the recognition I get.
   d. Nobody pays attention as long as I get my work done. I like it like that.
   e. I feel like a nameless, faceless nobody.
   f. Other _____.

3. Jesus chose all twelve apostles to "be with Him and that He might send them out to preach and to have authority to drive out demons" (Mk 3:14-15). How do you imagine James, Simon, and Judas felt about being selected for those tasks?

4. What individual contributions do you think a quiet man (James), a passionate man (Simon), and a compassionate man (Judas) may have made to the mix of personalities in the apostolic community?

5. How was the commission Jesus gave the apostles in Acts 1:8 similar to and different from their mission spelled out in Mark 3:14-15?

6. What roles did James, Simon, and Judas play on the day of Pentecost? How did their roles compare to those of the prominent apostles?

7. What is the relationship of James, Simon, and Judas to the church of Jesus Christ from Pentecost to the present time (Eph 2:20)? What will be their eternal relationship to the New Jerusalem (Rv 21:14)?

8. What encouragement do you draw from the importance of these anonymous apostles to the church of Jesus Christ?

9. How do these anonymous apostles challenge you to spend time with Jesus and faithfully fulfill your ministry?

GOING DEEPER

10. What are the internal and external barriers quiet people have to deal with to serve the Lord effectively?

11. What are the internal and external barriers passionate, cause-driven people have to deal with to serve the Lord effectively?

12. What are the internal and external barriers compassionate, emotionally sensitive people have to deal with to serve the Lord effectively?

CARING TIME

The kingdom of God includes no unimportant people. Jesus has a mission for each of us. Sometimes our greatest barriers to serving Him are inside of us. We assume we have nothing to offer Him (or we insist on being the star of the show). James, Simon, and Judas illustrate how Jesus takes greater delight in dependability than star ability.

1. How do you classify yourself?
   a. Quick
   b. Passsionate
   c. Compassionate
   d. Other. Please explain

2. How do our diverse tempermants compliment one another?

3. What internal and external barriers to serving the Lord effectively do you wrestle with most often?

4. How can we pray for you that you might better fill your role in Christ's church?

NEXT WEEK

Next week we turn our attention to Judas Iscariot, the chosen apostle who turned away from Jesus and betrayed Him. He did not learn that all that glitters is not gold. How could a man called to be with Jesus end up filled with Satan? Why did Jesus ever choose him? Judas serves as a chilling warning. "No one can be a slave of two masters, since either he will hate one and love the other, or be devoted to one and despise the other" (Mt 6:24).

Mk 3:13 He went up the mountain. Luke 6:12 recounts that Jesus prayed all night on the mountain preparing himself to choose the twelve.

Lk 6:12-13 Compare Matthew 10:3-4 and Mark 3:18 for the variant on the name Judas (Thaddaeus) and a different order for his and Simon the Zealot's names.

NOTES ON ACTS 1:4A, 7-8, 2:1-7A, 11B

1:4 the Father's promise. The Holy Spirit is the gift (Is 32:15; Jl 2:28-32; Lk 11:13; 12:12; 24:49; Gl 3:14). Jesus quoted the words of John the Baptist (Lk 3:16) as a reminder that from the very beginning the expectation was that through Him the Spirit of God would be poured out on all people.

1:8 The mission of Jesus was continued through the work of His Spirit empowering and enabling the disciples to bear witness to Him (Mt 28:19-20; Lk 12:11-12). The result of this empowering would be the spread of the gospel throughout the world from the spiritual heart of Israel (Jerusalem) to the immediate vicinity (Judea), to the despised Samaritans in the adjacent province to the north, to the outermost reaches of the earth.

2:1 the day of Pentecost. This was the Feast of Weeks (Ex 23:16; Lv 23:15-21; Dt 16:9-12) held 50 days after Passover. Originally a kind of thanksgiving day for gathered crops, it came to be associated with the commemoration of the giving of the Law at Mount Sinai (Ex 20:1-17). Jewish tradition held that when God gave the Law to Moses, a single voice spoke which was heard by all the nations of the world in their own language. Luke may be alluding to that in this story. Pentecost was a celebration in which thousands of the Jews from all over the empire would participate.

2:2-4 The Greek word for "wind" and "spirit" is the same, hence the symbolism of the Spirit coming like a great wind. Fire was often associated with divine appearances (Ex 3:2; 19:18). John the Baptist said Jesus would baptize His followers with the Holy Spirit and fire (Lk 3:16), symbolizing the cleansing, purifying effect of the Spirit. What is important here is that tongues served as a sign to the crowds of a supernatural event, the point of which was Jesus Christ.

2:4 filled with the Holy Spirit. This phrase is found elsewhere (Ac 4:8,31; 13:52; Eph 5:18), indicating a repeatable experience. Here, however, it was clearly associated with the baptism of the Spirit (Ac 1:5) which is an experi-

LESSON 9

ence new converts enter into upon acceptance of Jesus as the Messiah (Ac 11:15-16; 1 Co 12:13).

2:5-7a The disciples apparently made their way to the temple where they attracted a large crowd that was puzzled over how the apostles could speak in their native dialects.

NOTES ON EPHESIANS 2:19-22; REVELATION 21:9-14

Eph 2:19 foreigners. Nonresident aliens were disliked by the native population and often held in suspicion. **strangers.** These were residents of a foreign land. They paid taxes, but had no legal standing and few rights. **fellow citizens.** Whereas once the Gentiles had been "excluded from the citizenship of Israel" (v. 12), now they were members of God's kingdom. **members of God's household.** In fact, their relationship was far more intimate. They had become family.

2:20 cornerstone. The stone which rested firmly on the foundation and anchored two walls together, giving each its correct alignment.

2:21 fitted together. A term used by a mason to describe how two stones were prepared so that they would bond tightly together. **holy sanctuary.** The new sanctuary is not like the old temple, carved out of dead stone – beautiful but forbidding and exclusive. Rather, it is alive all over the world, inclusive of all, and made up of the individuals in whom God dwells.

Rev 21:14 the 12 names of the Lamb's 12 apostles. The very foundation of the city rests on the apostles of Jesus (Eph 2:20). The church was the result of the labors of the Twelve following the death and resurrection of Jesus. With the names of the 12 tribes at the gates and the 12 apostles at the foundation, it is clear that the New Jerusalem encompasses the believers of the Old Testament and the believers of the New Testament. All of God's people will have a place here.

Personal Notes

Judas Iscariot: All That Glitters Is Not Gold

Last Week

Last week we sketched what little we know about James the son of Alphaeus, Simon the zealot, and Judas the son of James. These nearly anonymous apostles form part of the foundation of the church. Their names will eternally grace the foundation of the New Jerusalem.

These little known apostles spent time with Jesus, overcame demons in His name, and preached the good news of the kingdom of God. They did it without human recognition to receive a divine "well done, good and faithful slave!" (Mt 25:21).

This week we look at the dark portrait of Judas Iscariot. Unlike the three apostles from last week, Judas has received a lot of attention through the centuries. Unfortunately, the Lord's last words to him will be "Depart from Me, you who are cursed, into the eternal fire prepared for the Devil and his angels!" (v. 41).

Ice-Breaker

Children don't need to learn greed; they need to learn to share. "Mine" is every young child's second favorite word, right after "No!" We understand and tolerate selfishness and greed in the very young. Soon, however, he or she receives a non-stop string of messages that sharing is good and selfishness is bad. Unchecked selfishness and greed cause all kinds of trouble for older children. They create incredible disaster for adults.

1. Which of these best reflects how you tried to get what you wanted from your parents when you were in short pants?
   a. Whining works wonders.
   b. Wear 'em down. Never take no for an answer.
   c. Tantrums.
   d. Divide and conquer, usually start with mom.
   e. Beg – "Please, please, pretty please."
   f. Other _____.

2. Mr. Potter was the greediest man in Bedford Falls according to It's a Wonderful Life. Who are some other greedy characters from stories or

movies? What impact did greed have on their lives and relationships?

3. When was the first time in your life that you remember feeling betrayed? How did you respond?

BIBLICAL FOUNDATION

The name Iscariot that attaches to Judas (Mt. 26:14) and his father Simon (Jn 13:2) referred to where they came from. Iscariot approximates the Hebrew expression *ish kerioth,* "man from Kerioth." Scholars debate the location of Kerioth. It probably was a town in southern Judea. All the other apostles came from Galilee. Attaching the label Iscariot to Judas identified him as the sole non-Galilean in the group.

Judas Iscariot appears in several biblical passages. Matthew, Mark, and Luke reported his betrayal of Christ without comment. Only John chose to pull back the curtain a little more and reveal a glimpse of what motivated the betrayer.

Never a True Believer
⁶⁶ From that moment many of His disciples turned back and no longer accompanied Him. ⁶⁷ Therefore Jesus said to the Twelve, "You don't want to go away too, do you?" ⁶⁸ Simon Peter answered, "Lord, who will we go to? You have the words of eternal life. ⁶⁹ We have come to believe and know that You are the Holy One of God!" ⁷⁰ Jesus replied to them, "Didn't I choose you, the Twelve? Yet one of you is the Devil!" ⁷¹ He was referring to Judas, Simon Iscariot's son, one of the Twelve, because he was going to betray Him.

John 6:66-71

A Slave of Greed
³ Then Mary took a pound of fragrant oil—pure and expensive nard—anointed Jesus' feet, and wiped His feet with her hair. So the house was filled with the fragrance of the oil. ⁴ Then one of His disciples, Judas Iscariot (who was about to betray Him), said, ⁵ "Why wasn't this fragrant oil sold for 300 denarii and given to the poor?" ⁶ He didn't say this because he cared about the poor but because he was a thief. He was in charge of the money-bag and would steal part of what was put in it.

John 12:3-6

Treachery Afoot
¹⁴ Then one of the Twelve—the man called Judas Iscariot—went to the chief priests ¹⁵ and said, "What are you willing to give me if I hand Him over to you?" So they weighed out 30 pieces of silver for him. ¹⁶ And from that time he started looking for a good opportunity to betray Him.

Matthew 26:14-16

² Now by the time of supper, the Devil had already put it into the heart of Judas, Simon Iscariot's son, to betray Him. ³ Jesus knew that the Father had given everything into His hands, that He had come from God, and that He was going back to God. ⁴ So He got up from supper, laid aside His robe, took a towel, and tied it around Himself. ⁵ Next, He poured water into a basin and began to wash His disciples' feet and to dry them with the towel tied around Him. ¹² When Jesus had washed their feet and put on His robe, He reclined again and said to them, "Do you know what I have done for you? . . . ¹⁵ For I have given you an example that you also should do just as I have done for you. . . . ¹⁷ If you know these things, you are blessed if you do them. ¹⁸ I'm not speaking about all of you; I know those I have chosen. But the Scripture must be fulfilled: The one who eats My bread has raised his heel against Me." . . . ²⁶ Jesus replied, "He's the one I give the piece of bread to after I have dipped it." When He had dipped the bread, He gave it to Judas, Simon Iscariot's son. ²⁷ After [Judas ate] the piece of bread, Satan entered him. Therefore Jesus told him, "What you're doing, do quickly." ²⁸ None of those reclining at the table knew why He told him this. ²⁹ Since Judas kept the money-bag, some thought that Jesus was telling him, "Buy what we need for the festival," or that he should give something to the poor. ³⁰ After receiving the piece of bread, he went out immediately. And it was night.

John 13:2-5, 12, 15, 17-18, 26-30

Betrayal
⁴⁷ While He was still speaking, Judas, one of the Twelve, suddenly arrived. A large mob, with swords and clubs, was with him from the chief priests and elders of the people. ⁴⁸ His betrayer had given them a sign: "The One I kiss, He's the One; arrest Him!" ⁴⁹ So he went right up to Jesus and said, "Greetings, Rabbi!"—and kissed Him. ⁵⁰ "Friend," Jesus asked him, "why have you come?" Then they came up, took hold of Jesus, and arrested Him.

Matthew 26:47-50

Self-Destruction
³ Then Judas, His betrayer, seeing that He had been condemned, was full of remorse and returned the 30 pieces of silver to the chief priests and elders. ⁴ "I have sinned by betraying innocent blood," he said. "What's that to us?" they said. "See to it yourself!" ⁵ So he threw the silver into the sanctuary and departed. Then he went and hanged himself. ⁶ The chief priests took the silver and said, "It's not lawful to put it into the temple treasury, since it is blood money." ⁷ So they conferred together and bought the potter's field with it as a burial place for foreigners.

Matthew 27:3-6

¹⁸ Now this man acquired a field with his unrighteous wages; and falling headfirst, he burst open in the middle, and all his insides spilled out. ¹⁹ This became known to all the residents of Jerusalem, so that in their own language that field is called Hakeldama, that is, Field of Blood.

Acts 1:18-19

PRINCIPLE DEVELOPMENT

Judas seems to have been a man driven by greed. When he sensed that his hope of becoming wealthy as a close associate of "King Jesus" was slipping away, he turned on Jesus and betrayed Him for thirty pieces of silver. When the authorities seized, beat, and sentenced Jesus to death, remorse overcame Judas; and he took his own life. What are we to learn from Judas' life?

PRINCIPLE 1

GREED IS A NORMAL TEMPTATION THAT WE ALL FACE, AND WE MUST BE ON GUARD AGAINST IT.

John's Gospel portrays Judas as a false disciple (6:70) who acted a part in order to steal money given to support Jesus and His apostles (12:6). Eventually Judas' love of money became a door into his soul through which Satan gained access and took control (13:2, 27). Paul may, among others, have had Judas Iscariot in mind when he wrote these words to Timothy: "For the love of money is a root of all kinds of evil, and by craving it, some have wandered away from the faith and pierced themselves with many pains" (1 Ti 6:10).

Having money isn't wrong. Working hard to gain wealth isn't wrong. As long as a Christian submits his use of wealth to the lordship of Christ, wealth can be a positive thing. Wisely invested wealth can fund projects for the kingdom of God that ordinary givers could never support. But as soon as the desire for wealth begins to dictate ethical compromises and value realignments, a Christian man is in deep spiritual trouble. Wealth makes a good servant but a lousy master.

PRINCIPLE 2

WHEN IT COMES TO MATERIAL POSSESSIONS, SATAN UNDERSTANDS OUR VULNERABILITY MORE THAN WE DO; AND HE TARGETS US IN THIS AREA OF OUR LIVES.

Satan even tempted Jesus in this area when he offered Him "all the kingdoms of the world and their splendor" if He would "fall down and worship" him (Mt 4:8-9). He ensnared and destroyed Judas Iscariot with greed for possessions. He will tempt you and me this way, too. Our culture promotes conspicuous consumption. One has to be intentionally counter-cultural not to long for wealth and possessions.

We don't know when Judas Iscariot began to want money more than the Lord. We don't know when he started pretending to care about God's kingdom and righteousness to get access to money meant to expand the kingdom. Perhaps Judas thought he was a true disciple with a greed problem that he would conquer some day.

By hypocritically concealing his sin of greed for a long time, Judas hardened his heart against all the appeals of God's grace. In the end he would not confess and repent of betraying Jesus either. He destroyed himself, remorseful but unrepentant.

PRINCIPLE 3

BECAUSE GOD IS PATIENT WITH US WHEN WE VIOLATE HIS WILL, WE MUST NOT INTERPRET HIS UNCONDITIONAL LOVE AS APPROVAL OF OUR SINFUL LIFESTYLE.

Jesus loved Judas until the very end. He never exposed him as a thief but waited for him to respond to His love. Eventually, Judas paid a horrible price for his sin. Paul wrote; "Don't be deceived: God is not mocked. For whatever a man sows he will also reap" (Ga 6:7).

If we persist in sin, God will eventually discipline us to draw us back into His will. We must be cautious however. God's "rope of mercy" is long. Sometimes we may convince ourselves that we can "get away" with our sin indefinitely. When God suddenly "tightens the noose" and our secret shame is exposed, the loss of reputation and trust can be very painful.

Finally, we must never allow Satan to convince us it's too late to seek forgiveness. Judas believed that lie. The apostle John told the truth: "If we confess our sins, He is faithful and righteous to forgive us our sins and to cleanse us from all unrighteousness" (1 Jn 1:9).

QUESTIONS FOR INTERACTION

1. What's the worst experience with betrayal that you have known as an adult? What was its impact on you?

2. What sort of mixed emotions do you imagine Jesus felt as He called Judas Iscariot to be an apostle?

3. In John 6:66-71, Jesus offered the Twelve a chance to leave Him, Peter affirmed great faith in Him, and Jesus revealed Satan's presence in the group. How do you imagine Judas reacted to each of these actions?

4. In the narrative of the anointing of Jesus' feet, what do you learn about Mary? What do you learn about Judas?

5. What can you infer about the intentionality and carefulness of Judas' hypocrisy from the fact that none of the other apostles suspected he was false?

6. How do you think Judas opened himself to evil to the extent that the devil could put things in his heart and then enter him (Jn 13:2, 27)?

7. How do you see Jesus reaching out to Judas, offering him opportunities to repent before and during his betrayal?

8. What makes Judas' kiss such an awful sign of betrayal (Mt 26:49)?

9. Emotionally speaking, why did Judas kill himself? Spiritually speaking, why did Judas kill himself?

10. How can greed turn a person into a hypocrite and false friend in today's world?

GOING DEEPER

11. How might the Gospel account have come out differently if Judas had repented of his betrayal of Jesus?

12. How do you think Judas' selfishness and greed interfered with any desire he may have had to repent?

13. How does greed open us to Satan and close us to Christ?

CARING TIME

We mustn't allow covetousness and greed any place in our lives. Satan loves to find these chinks in our spiritual armor and wriggle through them into our hearts. The apostle John advised: "Do not love the world or the things that belong to the world. If anyone loves the world, love for the Father is not in him. Because everything that belongs to the world – the lust of the flesh, the lust of the eyes, and the pride in one's lifestyle – is not from the Father, but is from the world" (1 Jn 2:15-16).

1. When do you find the devil tempting you to want more: money or possessions?

2. Do you find that other family members place a different value on money and possessions than you do? What problems, if any, does that create for you?

3. How can we hold one another accountable to keep money in its place and prevent greed from deceiving us?

NEXT WEEK

Next week we come upon the least familiar apostle. In Acts 1, the surviving eleven apostles selected a replacement for Judas Iscariot who had hanged himself. Matthias appears in one paragraph at the end of Acts 1 and vanishes from the pages of the New Testament. Some have suggested that Peter and the others erred in replacing Judas. They argue that God intended Paul to become the twelfth apostle. However, Paul had not been with Jesus from the beginning, although we've seen in the final chapter, he was indeed an apostle on the same level as the twelve. Matthias' quiet, steady faithfulness marked him as God's chosen servant.

NOTES ON JOHN 6:66-71

6:68 You have the words of eternal life. Peter had grasped the meaning of Jesus' interpretation of the feeding of the 5,000 (v 63).

NOTES ON JOHN 12:3-6

12:6 he was a thief. John's point was not to dismiss legitimate caring for the poor, but to point out that in spite of his words Judas' motives were self-serving.

LESSON 10

26:15 30 pieces of silver. This was not a very large amount (Zch 11:12), roughly 120 denarii. First century Palestinian laborers received a denarius for a day's work, so this amounted to four months' wages.

Notes on John 13:2-5, 12, 15, 17-18, 26-30

13:18 the Scripture must be fulfilled. Jesus quoted Psalm 41:9 as an example of a person being turned against by former friends. Like David, Jesus faced betrayal by His friends and counselors. The one who eats My bread has raised his heel against Me. Eating together was a sign of friendship. To lift up one's heel was a gesture of contempt, implying a desire to trample the other person underfoot.

13:26 He gave it to Judas. Although this was a signal that Judas was the betrayer, it may also have been Jesus' final attempt to call Judas back to Himself, since the sharing of food was a common sign of friendship and peace.

13:27 Satan entered him. The relationship between Satan's activity and that of Judas himself is never explained. On the one hand, it was his free choice to betray Jesus for whatever motives he had; on the other hand, in so doing he was following the desires of his spiritual father and lord, the devil. ***What you're doing, do quickly.*** Jesus' control of the timing of His death is manifest even in Judas' betrayal.

13:29 some thought. This signal escaped the awareness of the disciples.

Notes on Matthew 26:47-50

26:50 arrested Him. No charge was given. Perhaps it was blasphemy (9:3), violation of the Sabbath (12:2, 10, 14), or the practice of sorcery (9:34).

Notes on Matthew 27:3-6

27:3 full of remorse. Some think Judas went to the Sanhedrin not so much to get Jesus killed as to initiate the new order of freedom from Rome. Whatever Judas' rationale, he became "full of remorse" when Jesus did not overpower, but submitted to, the arresting force

LESSON 10

MATTHIAS: PRIVACY TO PROMINENCE

LAST WEEK

Last week Judas Iscariot's greed and treachery sobered us. We can only spec-ulate what Judas hoped he would gain from following Jesus; but when it didn't materialize, he began to steal from the fund that supported Jesus' ministry. His hollow, false heart became a chamber Satan could enter. Greed served as the key. Satan prompted Judas to betray Jesus. Then Satan betrayed Judas to a flood of remorse that prompted him to commit suicide.

This week we move outside the original apostolic band and look at the successor of Judas. Matthias had followed Jesus as long as Judas or any of the other apostles. He had witnessed all Jesus said and did. Most importantly, he had seen the resurrected Lord. Matthias did what Judas could never have. He effectively spread the gospel as a co-laborer with the other eleven apostles. And the Spirit lifted him from private servant-hood to prominent leadership.

ICE-BREAKER

Making choices is serious business. We've cared about how to choose all our lives – how to choose teams, how to choose friends, how to choose a college, a career, a wife, a church, a town, and a house to live in. The series of life choices goes on until someone else chooses the suit and the casket to bury us in.

1. How did you feel about "choosing up sides" to play ball games in gym or in your neighborhood?
   a. Loved it. I was usually a captain who chose.
   b. Great. I was usually one of the first chosen.
   c. Okay. I enjoyed playing.
   d. Not so hot. I was one of the kids they rounded up to make the teams even.
   e. I hated it. Nobody wanted me on his team. Everybody made fun of me.
   f. Other _____.

2. What position that you were chosen to fill made you proudest at the time? Why were you so pleased?

BIBLICAL FOUNDATION

Jesus chose twelve apostles. That made sense to all of their Jewish minds. There had been twelve sons of Jacob and twelve tribes of Israel. On one occasion Jesus told the apostles, "I assure you: In the Messianic Age, when the Son of Man sits on His glorious throne, you who have followed Me will also sit on 12 thrones, judging the 12 tribes of Israel" (Mt 19:28).

When Judas Iscariot killed himself, only eleven apostles remained. Eleven was a defective number. Some action had to be taken to complete the full complement of apostles. In the days following the ascension of Jesus, the eleven apostles "united in prayer, along with the women, including Mary the mother of Jesus, and His brothers" (Ac 1:14). They were waiting, in obedience to Jesus' instruction, for the promised Holy Spirit (vv 4-5). While they waited, God moved in the heart of Peter.

Qualified and Divinely Chosen

12 Then they returned to Jerusalem from the mount called Olive Grove, which is near Jerusalem—a Sabbath day's journey away. 13 When they arrived, they went to the room upstairs where they were staying:

Peter, John,
James, Andrew,
Philip, Thomas,
Bartholomew, Matthew,
James the son of Alphaeus,
Simon the Zealot, and Judas the son of James.

14 All these were continually united in prayer, along with the women, including Mary the mother of Jesus, and His brothers. 15 During these days Peter stood up among the brothers—the number of people who were together was about 120—and said: 16 "Brothers, the Scripture had to be fulfilled that the Holy Spirit through the mouth of David spoke in advance about Judas, who became a guide to those who arrested Jesus. 17 For he was one of our number and was allotted a share in this ministry. . . . 20 "For it is written in the Book of Psalms:

Let his dwelling become desolate;
let no one live in it; and
Let someone else take his position.

21 "Therefore, from among the men who have accompanied us during the whole time the Lord Jesus went in and out among us — 22 beginning from the baptism of John until the day He was taken up from us—from among these, it is necessary that one become a witness with us of His resurrection." 23 So they proposed two: Joseph, called Barsabbas, who was also known as Justus, and Matthias. 24 Then they

prayed, "You, Lord, know the hearts of all; show which of these two You have chosen ²⁵ to take the place in this apostolic service that Judas left to go to his own place." ²⁶ Then they cast lots for them, and the lot fell to Matthias. So he was numbered with the 11 apostles.

Acts 1:12-17, 20-26

PRINCIPLE DEVELOPMENT

Matthias, a man who is never mentioned by name in the Gospels and only in connection with one event in the book of Acts, suddenly became one of the Twelve Apostles (Ac 1:26). From that moment until his death as a martyr he helped unveil a great mystery that "was not made known to people in other generations"(Eph 3:5). That mystery consisted of the church, the body of Jesus Christ (v 10), a movement that has changed the course of human history.

PRINCIPLE I

GOD IS AN OMNISCIENT, SOVEREIGN PERSON WHO MAKES CHOICES AND USES METHODS AND MEANS THAT ONLY HE UNDERSTANDS.

When the Lord chose Matthias to replace Judas, He blessed a method that was even used among the pagans. Haman cast lots to determine when to destroy the Jews when they were in bondage to King Xerxes (Est 3:7). The Roman soldiers cast lots for Jesus' garments after He had been crucified (Mt 27:35). When the apostles used this method, they combined it with prayer. God honored this approach and selected Matthias, the man He had already chosen before time began.

Sometimes God achieves His purposes in unusual ways, simply because He is the sovereign God. He always knew that Judas would betray Jesus for thirty pieces of silver and that he would end up in a Christ-less eternity. Yet He chose him to be one of the apostles. He also knew that Matthias would replace Judas and had chosen him for this position before He ever created the world (Ro 9:22-24). Only God understands these divine mysteries. Only He can make these decisions, yet be just and fair.

THE OMNISCIENT AND SOVEREIGN GOD WHO MAKES ETERNAL CHOICES HAS DESIGNED HIS CHURCH IN SUCH A WAY THAT LEADERS ARE TO BE CHOSEN ON THE BASIS OF CHRISTIAN CHARACTER.

God's choice of Matthias to replace Judas illustrates a unique transitional moment. Matthias was highly qualified in terms of character. When Jesus chose the original Twelve, He worked with what He had. With a few exceptions, these men lacked character, and Jesus spent over three years "discipling them" and preparing them to carry out the Great Commission.

Peter, who began as a tough-minded businessman, became one of God's greatest servants. James was power-hungry but became the first Christian martyr. John was terribly self-centered but was transformed into the great apostle of love. Philip stopped allowing his pragmatic nature to interfere with his faith. Matthew turned from his materialism to seek God's kingdom first. Thomas became a transformed pessimist and operated as an eternal optimist. Simon left the Jewish Zealots and became a "zealot" for Jesus Christ.

Jesus had shaped Matthias' character before he became an apostle. From this point forward, leaders for the church were chosen on the basis of proven rather than potential character. The seven men designated to care for the Grecian widows were chosen because they were "men of good reputation, full of the Spirit and wisdom" (Ac 6:3). Stephen earned special recognition as "a man full of faith and the Holy Spirit" (v 5). The apostles and elders of the church in Jerusalem sent Barnabas to Antioch to help establish the first Gentile church on the basis that "he was a good man, full of the Holy Spirit and of faith" (11:24). The Pastoral Epistles outline the character qualities to be used in selecting spiritual leaders for individual congregations (1 Tm 3:1-7; Ti 1:5-9).

QUESTIONS FOR INTERACTION

1. How do you tend to feel when you're asked to do something you're not qualified to do? How do you tend to feel when you're asked to do something you are fully qualified to do?

2. Why do you suppose the Holy Spirit prompted Peter to be so restrictive about who could become the twelfth apostle (Ac 1:21-22)?

3. Why was it important in replacing Judas that the apostles and their associates had "continually united in prayer" for several days (Ac 1:14-15)?

4. Peter applied David's prayers concerning wicked men in general to Judas, the ultimate wicked man (Ac 1:16-17, 20). What points did Peter make from Psalm 69:25 and Psalm 109:8?

5. What was said about Judas, good and bad, in the course of the replacement procedure (Ac 1:16-17, 25)?

6. What qualifications did Peter lay down for the replacement of Judas (Ac 1:21-22)?

7. Why did they cast lots to choose Matthias rather than electing or appointing him (Ac 1:24-25)?

8. If, like Matthias, you had witnessed the whole ministry of Jesus from His baptism to His resurrection, what events or teachings would stand out to you? Why?

9. In the selection of Matthias to replace Judas, how do you see both responsible human choices and divine sovereignty at work?

GOING DEEPER

10. Why should we look for proven character before putting church leaders in office instead of trusting God to develop character after they take office?

11. How can we keep the selection of church leaders focused on spiritual issues rather than popularity and charisma?

12. What role does God play in the selection of our church leaders?

CARING TIME

The selection of Matthias to replace Judas Iscariot reminds us it's never too late to start getting ready for the time when The Great Conductor points to you to play lead instrument. Matthias invested more than three years of his life in being a private, committed Christ-follower. That had been an end in itself, but it became the means to an unforeseen greater end. Don't worry that you don't know what the future holds. Follow the Lord Jesus as closely you can, and you will find yourself equipped for whatever He has in mind for you. Be ready, so that when Jesus calls you out of obscurity, you'll be ready.

1. How has the Lord Jesus impacted your character development since you became a Christian?

2. What ministry roles do you fill in the church? What part did people play in choosing you for that ministry? What part did God play?

3. How can we encourage you or assist you in your ministry?

NEXT WEEK

Next week we move still further outside the original apostolic band to consider the life and ministry of Paul, the apostle to the Gentiles. Paul broke onto the scene in the book of Acts as a premeditated murderer and persecutor of the church. Despite this, we will see how the Lord chose Paul and commissioned him to fish for men. Jesus commissioned Paul as clearly as He called the Twelve. Finally we will note what happened when Jesus sent Paul fishing in a bigger pond for different kind of fish.

NOTES ON ACTS 1:12-17, 20-26

1:12 The Mount of Olives. Where the ascension occurred; is just outside of the city's eastern wall. The angels' message picked up on Zechariah 14:4, which teaches that the Messiah will one day appear on that mountain when He comes to fully establish His reign. *a Sabbath day's journey.* This phrase occurs only here in the Bible. Tradition restricted how far a Jew could travel on the Sabbath to about 1,000 yards (literally 2,000 cubits), the distance between the ark of the covenant and the Israelite camp as Israel wandered in the wilderness (Jos 3:4).

1:13 the room upstairs where they were staying. This probably was the same upstairs room in which Jesus washed the disciples' feet, delivered the Upper Room Discourse, and instituted the Lord's Supper on the night before His crucifixion (Mk 14:22-31; Jn 13 – 16). It must have been spacious to accommodate 120 people.

1:15 the number of people who were together was about 120. Most of the 120 would have been Galileans who came to Jerusalem with Jesus before the Passover. Several were women, some of whom financially underwrote the ministry of Jesus and the apostles (Lk 8:1-3). Perhaps the most notable addition to this circle of believers were the brothers of Jesus (Ac 1:14) who had not believed prior to His death and resurrection (Jn 7:5).

1:16 Scripture had to be fulfilled. After the resurrection, Jesus had shown the apostles how the Old Testament pointed to Him (Lk 24:27, 44). The Law and the prophets would become an important resource for the apostles to understand Him and their mission all the more.

1:20 Let his dwelling become desolate . . . . Peter quoted two psalms. The first citation is Psalm 69:25 in which David prayed for the ruin of his enemies. Peter applied it to Judas' removal from apostleship. ***Let someone else . . .*** Here Peter cited Psalm 109:8, another instance in which David prayed against those who were "wicked and deceitful" (v 2). Peter used it as rationale for replacing Judas, the ultimate wicked and deceitful man.

1:22 from the baptism of John until the day He was taken up from us. Since the apostles were to bear witness to all Jesus said and did, it was important that they all be people who had been involved from the very beginning.

1:23 Joseph, called Barsabbas, who was also known as Justus. This disciple's name was Joseph, which meant "May he add" (see Gn 30:24). He had earned the nickname Barsabbas, "Son of the Sabbath," probably on the basis of his piety. Justus was a Latin name. Many Jews used a non-Hebrew name when dealing with Gentiles (compare Saul/Paul). ***Matthias.*** This is another form of the name Matthew. Matthias and Matthew both meant "Gift of the Lord." Joseph and Matthias may have been two of the seventy disciples Jesus sent to preach and heal (Lk 10:1, 17). Different traditions place Matthias in ministry in Judea, where he was stoned by Jews, and in Ethiopia, where he was crucified by Gentiles.

1:26 cast lots. "Lots" are referred to seventy times in the Old Testament and seven times in the New. Many of these events occurred before most of the Bible was revealed to give guidance. In spite of all these references, we know nothing about what lots physically looked like, whether they were marked stones, sticks of different lengths, some kind of dice, or something else entirely. Lots could select one from a large group (Jnh 1:7), arrange a group (1 Ch 25:8-31), or determine, as in this case, an "either-or" choice.

Personal Notes

PAUL: MURDERER TURNED MISSIONARY

LAST WEEK

Last week we looked at the least familiar of the apostles, Matthias. Peter led the disciples gathered in the upstairs room in determining from the Old Testament that another should complete the apostolic number and ministry. Matthias had witnessed the miracles and teaching of Jesus from the time of His baptism until His ascension into heaven. God personally selected Matthias by lot, moving from privacy to prominence.

This week we turn to the apostle Paul. Unlike Matthias, Paul had no contact we know of with Jesus during His earthly life. In fact, Paul (called Saul at that time) hated the name and the followers of Jesus until he bumped into Jesus in a blazing encounter on the road to Damascus. A murderer instantly became a missionary for Jesus.

ICE-BREAKER

Before the larger world knew him as Paul, the Jews of Tarsus and Jerusalem called him Saul. Saul was on a fast track to prominence in first-century Judaism. He made opposition to the Jewish sect known as "The Way" his signature issue. Saul became a fanatical persecutor of these followers of Jesus who would one day be called Christians. Webster's Collegiate Dictionary says a fanatic is someone "marked by excessive enthusiasm and often intense uncritical devotion" to something. Most of us have been harmlessly fanatical about something at one time or another.

1. About which of the following have you been at least a little fanatical at some time? Describe your fanaticism.
   a. Football, baseball, basketball, hockey, or another sport.
   b. Fords, Chevys, or some other kind of car.
   c. Girls.
   d. Guns or the glory of war.
   e. Airplanes.
   f. A hobby.
   g. A job.
   h. Other _____.

2. When have you found yourself trying to reason with a fanatic who would not listen to reason touching his or her pet idea? What was the experience like?

BIBLICAL FOUNDATION

Saul of Tarsus was no doubt named after Saul, the first king of Israel (1 Sm 9:1-2, 17; 10:23-24). King Saul had been the most famous Benjaminite in the Old Testament. The parents of Saul of Tarsus must have had lofty ambitions for their son. They sent him to Jerusalem for the best education a future Jewish leader could receive (Ac 22:3). The Bible calls him "a young man" at the time Stephen was martyred (Ac 7:58). He may been poised to begin his career. Like many Jews who interacted with Gentiles regularly, Saul used a non-Jewish name during those contacts. The Gentiles knew him as Paul.

Hebrew of the Hebrews
If anyone else thinks he has grounds for confidence in the flesh, I have more: [5] circumcised the eighth day; of the nation of Israel, of the tribe of Benjamin, a Hebrew born of Hebrews; as to the law, a Pharisee; [6] as to zeal, persecuting the church; as to the righteousness that is in the law, blameless.

Philippians 3:4b-6

[3] He continued, "I am a Jewish man, born in Tarsus of Cilicia, but brought up in this city at the feet of Gamaliel, and educated according to the strict view of our patriarchal law. Being zealous for God, just as all of you are today...."

Acts 22:3

Zealous Persecutor
[1] Saul agreed with putting him to death.
  On that day a severe persecution broke out against the church in Jerusalem, and all except the apostles were scattered throughout the land of Judea and Samaria. [2] But devout men buried Stephen and mourned deeply over him. [3] Saul, however, was ravaging the church, and he would enter house after house, drag off men and women, and put them in prison.

Acts 8:1-3

Conversion
[4] "I persecuted this Way to the death, binding and putting both men and women in jail, [5] as both the high priest and the whole council of elders can testify about me. Having received letters from them to the

brothers, I was traveling to Damascus to bring those who were prisoners there to be punished in Jerusalem. [6] "As I was traveling and near Damascus, about noon an intense light from heaven suddenly flashed around me. [7] I fell to the ground and heard a voice saying to me, 'Saul, Saul, why are you persecuting Me?' [8] I answered, 'Who are You, Lord?' "He said to me, 'I am Jesus the Nazarene, whom you are persecuting!' [9] Now those who were with me saw the light, but they did not hear the voice of the One who was speaking to me. [10] Then I said, 'What should I do, Lord?' And the Lord told me, 'Get up and go into Damascus, and there you will be told about everything that is assigned for you to do.' [11] Since I couldn't see because of the brightness of that light, I was led by the hand by those who were with me, and came into Damascus. [12] Someone named Ananias, a devout man according to the law, having a good reputation with all the Jews residing there, [13] came to me, stood by me, and said, 'Brother Saul, regain your sight.' And in that very hour I looked up and saw him. 14 Then he said, 'The God of our fathers has appointed you to know His will, to see the Righteous One, and to hear the sound of His voice. 15 For you will be a witness for Him to all people of what you have seen and heard. 16 And now, why delay? Get up and be baptized, and wash away your sins by calling on His name.' "

Acts 22:4-16

Preparation for Ministry

[15] But when God, who from my mother's womb set me apart and called me by His grace, was pleased [16] to reveal His Son in me, so that I could preach Him among the Gentiles, I did not immediately consult with anyone. [17] I did not go up to Jerusalem to those who had become apostles before me; instead I went to Arabia and came back to Damascus. [18] Then after three years I did go up to Jerusalem to get to know Cephas, and I stayed with him 15 days.

Galatians 1:15-18

Apostle to the Gentiles

[7] On the contrary, they saw that I had been entrusted with the gospel for the uncircumcised, just as Peter was for the circumcised. [8] For He who was at work with Peter in the apostleship to the circumcised was also at work with me among the Gentiles. [9] When James, Cephas, and John, recognized as pillars, acknowledged the grace that had been given to me, they gave the right hand of fellowship to me and Barnabas, [agreeing] that we should go to the Gentiles and they to the circumcised.

Galatians 2:7-9

²⁰ So my aim is to evangelize where Christ has not been named, in order that I will not be building on someone else's foundation, ²¹ but, as it is written: Those who had no report of Him will see, and those who have not heard will understand. ²² That is why I have been prevented many times from coming to you. ²³ But now I no longer have any work to do in these provinces, and I have strongly desired for many years to come to you ²⁴ whenever I travel to Spain. For I do hope to see you when I pass through, and to be sent on my way there by you, once I have first enjoyed your company for a while.

Romans 15:20-24

Motivation as an Apostle

¹² I give thanks to Christ Jesus our Lord, who has strengthened me, because He considered me faithful, appointing me to the ministry— ¹³ one who was formerly a blasphemer, a persecutor, and an arrogant man. Since it was out of ignorance that I had acted in unbelief, I received mercy, ¹⁴ and the grace of our Lord overflowed, along with the faith and love that are in Christ Jesus. ¹⁵ This saying is trustworthy and deserving of full acceptance: "Christ Jesus came into the world to save sinners"—and I am the worst of them. ¹⁶ But I received mercy because of this, so that in me, the worst [of them], Christ Jesus might demonstrate the utmost patience as an example to those who would believe in Him for eternal life.

1 Timothy 1:12-16

PRINCIPLE DEVELOPMENT

Before he put his faith in Christ, Paul was known as a tough-minded, no-nonsense, self-righteous Pharisee. After he professed Christian faith, other believers doubted his conversion for a long time. A number of years passed during which Paul studied and ministered in various locations. His story teaches us lessons about transformation and waiting for God to fulfill His purposes in His time.

PRINCIPLE 1

NO MATTER HOW SINFUL WE ARE, GOD'S GRACE EXTENDS TO ALL HUMANITY.

Paul classified himself as the worst of sinners because of his violent and cruel acts against Christians (1 Tm 1:15). He stated clearly, however, that God had mercy on him and would have mercy on anyone else who called out to Him, no matter how deeply they had become mired in sin (v 16).

Do you think your sin is too great to be forgiven? If so, think again of the apostle Paul. Don't let Satan deceive you into believing you cannot be saved because of your sinful lifestyle. The only unpardonable sin is rejecting Jesus Christ!

PRINCIPLE 2

GOD WORKS HIS GREATEST MIRACLE WHEN HE TRANSFORMS A PRACTIC-ING SINNER INTO A GODLY SAINT.

Paul was a murderer who became one of the greatest missionaries who ever lived. That was a stupendous miracle of God. True, it would have been wonderful to see Jesus multiply the loaves and fishes to feed five thousand men and their families. More wonderful would have been witnessing Paul receiving Jesus as the "bread of life" and inheriting eternal life.

At some point each apostle experienced this greatest miracle in his life. I trust that this miracle has happened to you, too. If it hasn't, you need to do what Paul did and bow before Jesus as your Savior and let Him start transforming your life from the inside out.

PRINCIPLE 3

ONCE WE BECOME CHRISTIANS, WE CAN OFTEN SEE HOW GOD HAS BEEN AT WORK IN OUR LIVES EVEN BEFORE WE PASSED FROM DEATH TO LIFE.

Before Paul was born, God had a plan for his life. All of his early education in Judaism and Greek and Roman thought and his studies under Gamaliel prepared him for the great task of becoming the apostle to the Gentiles. Once he became a Christian, Paul drew on all his education and experience to communicate the gospel effectively to both Jews and Gentiles.

Can you see how God can use your preconversion experiences to help you serve Him? No matter how difficult your past circumstances, He is able to make "all things work together for the good of those who love God: those who are called according to His purpose" (Rm 8:28).

PRINCIPLE 4

IT TAKES TIME TO BECOME PREPARED TO CARRY OUT GOD'S HIGHEST PURPOSE IN OUR LIVES.

Paul was a highly educated man when he became a Christian, but he was not ready to become an apostle to the Gentiles. He spent approximately ten years, both relearning what he already knew and discovering God's great plan for the church. Paul served God during that time. He preached and evangelized almost from the moment he met Jesus on the road outside Damascus. Even that was part of his preparation.

Then the Holy Spirit told the leaders of the church at Antioch to "set apart for Me Barnabas and Saul for the work that I have called them to" (Ac 13:2). During the next fifteen to twenty years of missionary endeavor Paul fulfilled his calling as the apostle to the Gentiles. God is preparing all of us for greater service. We must not get ahead of Him in terms of what we personally want to achieve. We should faithfully serve Him in every opportunity that presents itself. As we are faithful in every small thing, God may entrust us with a major ministry (Mt 25:21; Lk 16:10).

PRINCIPLE 5

THE GREATEST MOTIVATION FOR SERVING JESUS CHRIST SHOULD BE GOD'S LOVE AND GRACE IN SAVING US.

Paul never forgot God's mercy in saving him, the worst of sinners (1 Tm 1:15-16). He passed on this "motivational message" to all of us by writing these words to Titus:

For the grace of God has appeared, with salvation for all people, instructing us to deny godlessness and worldly lusts and to live in a sensible, righteous, and godly way in the present age, while we wait for the blessed hope and the appearing of the glory of our great God and Savior, Jesus Christ. He gave Himself for us to redeem us from all lawlessness and to cleanse for Himself a special people, eager to do good works (Ti 2:11-14).

QUESTIONS FOR INTERACTION

1. What's the biggest reversal of position you've ever made in your life? How hard was it for you to make that reversal?

2. What did Paul put his confidence in during his pre-Christian days?

3. What activities did Paul engage in when persecuting the church?

4. What steps did the Lord Jesus take Paul through in his conversion experience (Ac 22:6-16)?

5. Why do you think the Lord Jesus repeatedly told Paul that he had been persecuting Him (Ac 22:7-8)? Why would that have been news to Paul?

LESSON 12

6. Why would the Lord commission Paul to take the gospel to all people as part of his conversion?

7. From what sources did Paul get his confidence that he was to minister the gospel to the Gentiles (Gl 1:15-18; 2:7-9)?

8. What principle guided Paul's ever-widening sphere of missionary activity (Ro 15:20-24)?

9. What sin(s) are you most grateful that God in His mercy forgave through Christ's sacrifice for you?

10. What do you think is your special calling to fulfill in the body of Christ?

 GOING DEEPER

11. Do you have a pioneering spirit like Paul, or do you enjoy building on the work of others? How does that affect the way you serve in Christ's church?

12. How important do you think it was that Peter, James, and John approved of Paul's ministry to the Gentiles (Gl 2:7-9)?

13. How important is it for pioneers and builders to cooperate in the church today? Why do you think that way?

 CARING TIME

Paul was a man of vision and drive. He worked tirelessly to pursue his mission to preach the gospel of Jesus Christ to the Gentiles in regions where no one else had evangelized. Most of us are not wired to be focused world-beaters like Paul, but we all can benefit from reflecting on his example of a purpose-driven life.

1. Paul was motivated in his apostleship by an overwhelming sense of God's mercy that had delivered him from the sin of murdering Christians? What motivates you to serve the Lord?

2. What experiences, good and bad, from your pre-Christian days may make you a more effective or compassionate servant of Christ?

3. Who might we reach out to and invite to join our group for the next unit of study?

3:5 eighth day. On the eighth day after birth a Jewish boy (as opposed to a proselyte) was circumcised. Paul was a true Jew right from the time of his birth. ***the tribe of Benjamin.*** The members of the tribe of Benjamin constituted an elite group within Israel. ***a Pharisee.*** He was one of the spiritual elite of Israel.

3:6 as to zeal, persecuting the church. Zeal was a highly praised virtue among the Jews. Paul had demonstrated his zeal for the Law by ferreting out Christians and bringing them to trial (Ac 22:4-5; 26:9-11). ***blameless.*** To the best of his ability, Paul had tried to observe the whole Law.

Notes on Acts 22:3

22:3 a Jewish man . . . brought up in this city. Although a citizen of Tarsus by virtue of his birth, Paul spent much of his early life in Jerusalem. Chapter 23:16 implies that Paul's sister and her family lived in the city. ***Gamaliel.*** Gamaliel was a highly respected Pharisee, head of the Hillel wing of this sect. To have received an education from this man was to have had access to the best possible Jewish education (5:34). ***our patriarchal law.*** Paul emphasized that he, too, had a lifelong knowledge of and respect for the Law.

Notes on Acts 8:1-3

8:1-3 Whether Acts 26:10 is sufficient evidence that Paul belonged to the Sanhedrin is uncertain, but he quickly became the leading figure in a violent persecution of the church.

8:3 ravaging. This word is used to describe how a beast rips the flesh off its victim. Saul's persecution led to Christians being condemned to death as well (9:1-2).

Notes on Acts 22:4-16

22:4 this Way. Unique to Acts as a name for Christianity (19:9, 23; 24:14, 22).

Notes on Galatians 1:15-18

1:15 from my mother's womb set me apart. Paul's experience was similar to that of Old Testament prophets (Is 49:1-6; Jr 1:5). He could see the hand of God throughout his life.

1:16 among the Gentiles. With Paul's conversion came his commission to preach to the Gentiles (Ac 9:15). In encountering Christ, he came to the realization that the Law was bankrupt (insofar as its ability to save anyone).

LESSON 12

There was no barrier preventing Gentiles from coming to the all-sufficient Christ.

1:18 *after three years.* A significant interval of time elapsed between his conversion and his first visit to Jerusalem. ***Jerusalem.*** It took courage for Paul to return here, both to his former friends who might well try to harm him (because of his conversion to Christianity) and to new friends who might not even receive him (because of their suspicions about him). ***15 days.*** This was a short visit, and Paul spent much of his time preaching (Ac 9:28-29).

NOTES ON GALATIANS 2:7-8

2:7 *On the contrary.* In fact, they acknowledged his sphere of authority. ***for the uncircumcised.*** Though Paul often witnessed first to Jews (Ac 9:20; 26:20), his major mission was to the Gentiles (22:21).

NOTES ON ROMANS 15:20-24

15:24 *Spain.* The Roman colony of Spain was situated at the western edge of the civilized world, no doubt the reason Paul's pioneering spirit was drawn there.

NOTES ON 1 TIMOTHY 1:12-16

1:13 *one who was formerly.* Paul was utterly amazed that he, of all people, had been chosen for this high calling, given his past record. ***a blasphemer.*** Paul had denied Christ and tried to force others to do the same (Ac 26:11). ***a persecutor, and an arrogant man.*** He had actively opposed the church by searching out Christians, arresting them, throwing them in prison, even voting for their deaths. ***it was out of ignorance that I had acted in unbelief.*** Paul was not saying that he had received mercy because he was without guilt. All he was saying is that he acted "unintentionally" instead of "defiantly," using a common Old Testament distinction (Nm 15:22-31; Lk 23:34).

1:15 *Christ Jesus came into the world to save sinners.* By means of this quotation, Paul explained his own transformation (and gave Timothy hope for the transformation of the false teachers). The emphasis here is on the incarnation ("Jesus came intro the world") and redemption ("to save sinners). ***and I am the worst of them.*** The mention of sinners reminded Paul of his own state. He was overwhelmed by the magnitude of his sin and by the expansiveness of God's grace.